"Your Compl

MW01287207

STRATEGY
PLANNING & EXECUTION
FROM A TO Z

100'S OF COMMON WEAKNESSES & TIPS

Best Used Tools & Techniques
For a Winning Strategic Plan

✗ 100's of Common Weaknesses Highlighted
✓ 100's of Winning Solutions & Tips Provided

RACHAD BAROUDI PhD

DEDICATIONS

This book is dedicated to my family,
without whose support and love,
I would have not been able to write it.

FOREWORD

The key reason leaders care about strategy development is because they want to execute it well. Strategic decisions must be translated into tactical decisions that, in turn, become operational decisions. To successfully execute strategy, companies must link strategy development process to execution.

So, Dr. Rachad comes with another contribution to the body of knowledge "*Strategy Planning & Execution From A To Z*". This book is targeting strategy and performance professionals around the world. It has a great deal of detailed tips and solutions. Leaders had been developing and executing strategies for centuries, but with most common weaknesses highlighted here, there is a fairly high likelihood that they will do fewer mistakes in the future. Summarizing all what "To-Do" and what "Not-To-Do" in one book is an advantage. The author takes this a step further by closing the strategy loop from A to Z.

I appreciate the contribution Dr. Rachad have made to build upon existing tested and proven approaches to move the field of strategic planning and performance management forward in important new direction.

By Emir Mavani PhD
Policy & Strategy Advisor

Dr. Emir Mavani is a leading expert in government reform in Africa, Asia, and Malaysia. He undertook many "Strategic Diagnostic" projects in the telecoms, oil and gas, manufacturing, and financial sectors. In Malaysia, he gained his early experience in government modernization when he undertook various projects in administrative modernization area. In East Asia and Africa, he worked as a consultant for UNDP and the World Bank in public sector reforms and managed various international development projects. In UAE, he was the advisor to the Minister of Finance in the areas of governance and public budget reforms. Currently, Dr. Emir is the advisor for policy and strategy development for Abu Dhabi Government.

TABLE OF CONTENTS

PREFACE

The purpose of this book is to identify the critical factors that lead to successful strategic planning implementation. It highlights the reasons why some organizations effectively implement their strategic plan while many others fail to do so. In addition, it aims to inform the reader on various tools and techniques used in strategic planning cycle, from development stage to implementation stage.

According to a survey done by Palladium Group, 70% to 90% of organizations fail to successfully execute their strategies. There is a need for a simplified book such as this one to explore the whole strategic cycle to identify and document the *weaknesses* that lead to failed execution. In short, having an effective strategic planning and execution process is becoming increasingly critical in today's dynamic and integrated environment. Many past high-level articles and theories were written by authors with academic background. For this reason, this book fills the gap by introducing simple check lists that could be used by strategic planning and performance professionals to do their job more effectively.

All chapters covered in this book include writings on learned opinion concerning common *weaknesses* in strategic planning and implementation process from beginning to end. Special emphasis is placed upon the most critical factors that lead to successful implementation of the strategic plan. Historical work and studies done on evaluation of what factors most significantly influence the strategic planning process are highlighted. The views and opinions of modern management writers concerning strategic planning development, strategy methodology, strategy implementation, and related strategy automation tools are discussed. Together, the historical theories and modern approaches form a solid basis upon which a strong set of knowledge that helps to further refine the strategic planning process.

This book is divided into six chapters. Chapter one is an introduction to strategic planning and its current issues and challenges. Chapter two covers strategic planning development. Chapter three presents various strategic planning and monitoring methodologies. Chapter four covers strategic planning implementation. Chapter five talks about strategy management automation. Finally, chapter six includes the conclusion and summary of the main issues in strategic planning and implementation.

This book highlights many *weaknesses* that exist throughout strategic plan development and execution process. Some of the discussed *weaknesses* in details are; over-engineered or weak strategic plan; increasingly complex environment; weak leadership skills; strategic plan weak link to budget; usage of confusing and inconsistent terminology; unreasonable time period from planning to execution; lack of education and training of staff; lack of executive commitment; forced cascading approach; absence of IT strategy management tool; and finally management driven by short-term goals.

CHAPTER 1

INTRODUCTION

CHAPTER 1: INTRODUCTION

1.1 Strategic Planning Overview

Perhaps the most common theme in the planning literature is its obsession with control of decisions, strategies, and actions of workers and managers. In most cases, planning final aim is to control markets and customers. Henry Mintzberg wrote once that "Planning is an activity by which man in society endeavors to gain mastery to shape his collective future by power of his reason."[1] According to Dr. Robert Kaplan and Dr. David Norton planning "implies the movement of an organization from its present position to a desirable but uncertain future position."[2]

Many large and medium organizations today have "Corporate Planning Department" to ensure all activities are carefully planned. This also could be seen by others as an obsession with control to reflect a fear of uncertainty. According to Richard D. Young, Strategic planning is based on the premise that leaders and managers must be effective strategists if their organizations are to fulfill their missions, meet their mandates, and satisfy constituents in the years ahead[3]. Planners are not basically different from anyone else in this regard. Most humans fear uncertainty to some degree. One way to deal with this feeling of lack of control is to ensure no surprises, or in other words to seek control over anything that might surprise us. "Anything" here could mean behaviors, programs, activities, initiatives, and events. In a sense, reducing uncertainty is, or at least

---

1   Henry Mintzberg, The Pitfalls Of Strategic Planning, Fall, 1993, California Management Review.

2   Dr. Robert Kaplan & David Norton, Having Trouble With Your Strategy Then Map It, 10/1/2000, Harvard Business Review, pp.7-13

3   Richard D. Young, Perspectives on Strategic Planning in the Public Sector, 1/1/2003, Governmental Research with the Institute for Public Service and Policy Research, pp.1-28

has become the Planners' profession. In today's competitive business environment there is absolute need to prepare for contingencies and to minimize surprises. Michael Allen, General Electric's chief planner wrote once "The age of discontinuity had just dawned when General Electric started its strategic planning process."

The obsession with control could also lead to planning behaviors, or planning's attitude toward "turbulence" in the market place. One of the arguments states that planning has generally gained its greatest support when conditions have been relatively stable. It works best when it deals with realistic change within its existing scope. For instance, the process gained popularity initially during those 1960s that Makridakis described as years of such steady economic growth. On the contrary, planning deals less well with unstable, unpredictable situations. For example, it had its greatest setbacks when conditions changed unpredictably after the energy price increases of the 1970s.

Another argument against planning is that some organizations take advantage of the situations and turn them around to use as a tool, not because anyone necessarily believes in the value of the process but because influential outsiders do. This is when planning becomes a public relations game. Michael Porter was concerned about this issue, "Strategy had lost its intellectual currency. It was losing adherents. People were being tricked and misled by other ideas," he said [4]. This view of planning as a front wall to impress outsiders is supported by no shortage of evidence. Nutt cited those "city governments that hire consultants to do strategic planning to impress bond rating agencies," and "firms that posture with each other and the marketplace with their claims of long-range planning". Cohen and March described plans that "become symbols": for example, "an organization that is failing can announce a plan to succeed".

---

4   Keith Hammonds, You've got to make time for strategy, 3/1/2001, Illustrations, pp. 1-6

They also discussed plans that "become advertisements," noting that "what is frequently called a 'plan' by a university is really an investment brochure". Langley found this to be true in the public sector in general, where public relation was "probably a very common motivation for strategic planning," although the same kind of role is played by subsidiaries and/or divisions who have to produce 'strategic plans' for their parent firms. [5]

Strategic planning in the management and administrative context is a modern concept and process identifiable within both the corporate and public arenas[6]. Goodstein, Nolan, and Pfeiffer's definition of strategic planning takes us away from the notion that strategic planning is a staff job and focuses more on a process that requires the senior leaders of an organization to set its strategic direction.[7]

In a narrow sense, some planning for the purposes of public relations seems to be justified. After all, small businesses need their capital, developing nations their aid, and universities their support. But in a broader sense, is this kind of planning justified at all? Leaving aside waste of resources where money could be saved if everyone stopped playing this public relations game and where planning probably distorts priorities in the organization itself. In poor nations, for example, it misallocates skills that are in very short supply and capabilities that could be devoted to solving real problems.

Today, governments are faced with a far greater pressure for delivery and performance than ever before. It has been recognized that government has an enormous capacity to

5   Henry Mintzberg, The Pitfalls Of Strategic Planning, Fall, 1993, California Management Review, pp. 1-12

6   Richard D. Young, Perspectives on Strategic Planning in the Public Sector, 1/1/2003, Governmental Research with the Institute for Public Service and Policy Research, pp.1-28

7   Denise Lindsey Wells, Strategic Management for Senior Leaders - A Handbook for Implementation, 3/1/1996, Department of the Navy Total Quality Leadership Office, pp. 3-94

deliver real outcomes for society and to pursue objectives that can make a big difference to the quality of life of citizens. However, in order to do this, government must have some way of measuring the successes, failures and progress achieved in the pursuit of those objectives. Increasingly, strategic planning and performance management has been recognized as an important tool to ensure that government is capable of measuring its activities and feeding the results of that measurement back into a planning process to help improve future performance. Over the last decades, many countries around the world have been utilizing some kind of planning and performance management tools for their public sector agencies and local bodies. [8]

Clearly many government institutions have seen internally the benefit of planning and measurement. However, what has been unanswered is how much of these institutions are making a difference for societies that they are serving. It is not clear if societies are better off as a result of these government institution's efforts. Executives, managers, and employees in the government sector need to view planning and performance from a broader perspective. They require a system that not only counts the inputs and outputs of the system, but one that provides an opportunity to assess progress in reaching the institution's true mission. Strategic planning has risen to the challenge of the private sector and is equally well-equipped to facilitate a rapid and dramatic transition of 21st century government organizations.

In the private sector the measures appearing in the strategic plan could lead to improved bottom line performance. Improving shareholder value is the end result for profit seeking enterprises which are accountable to their financial stakeholders to do that. It is not the same in public organizations. Even though they are accountable for the efficient allocation of funds, they exist to serve a higher purpose such as increasing public safety. The key

8   Paul R. Niven, Primerus Consulting, Adapting The Balanced Scorecard To Fit The Public And Nonprofit Sectors, 4/22/2003, QPR, pp. 2-5

here is that they don't have total control to reach their mission. These organizations can influence the outcomes. However, it is only through planning and measurement that they are able to claim any real difference made in the lives of citizens. It is not common to achieve their mission overnight. Doing the planning, monitoring performance, and learning from the results will provide these organizations with short to medium-term information they require to achieve their mission.[9]

Strategic planning and performance management remain at the core of each organization, regardless of whether it's a city government, Fortune 500 company, or nonprofit institution. Government organizations often have a difficult time building a clear and brief strategy. While many attempts are made to develop statements of strategy, they end up listing programs and initiatives to secure dollars from funding bodies. Strategy is about those broad priorities to pursue in order to achieve a mission. The priorities must be consistent with one another in an effort to respond effectively and efficiently to surrounding challenges and opportunities. Once the strategy is developed, it serves as the guide for effective implementation. Consider the following quotes:[10]

> *"There is a profound feeling in the country [USA] that Government has not been doing its job – not just that tax dollars are wasted, but that Government cannot be counted on to improve the nation's future or support the current aspirations of ordinary Americans. This leads to the obvious question of whether the present government organization can operate effectively."(Senator John Glenn, 1993)*[11]

---

9   Robert S. Kaplan, "The Balanced Scorecard and Nonprofit Organizations," Balanced Scorecard Report, November-December, 2002. pp. 1-4.

10   Robert Mellor, Performance Measurement & Management In Asian-Pacific Local Government, 9/1/2003, The Network of Local Government Training and Research, pp. 2-69

11   Glenn, Senator John, excerpt from opening statements – United States Senate Committee on Governmental Affairs "Improving Government Performance and Organization, 1993, as cited in An Overview of Performance Measurement, ICMA/ Richard Fisher, ICMA website, USA, 2001

"Local Government provides a wide range of services to its constituents...through the provision of services, Local Government has a real effect on the standard and quality of living of people living and/or working within the Local Government area. Given this impact, it is important that these services are provided in an efficient manner and at an appropriate level of quality". (IPART, 1997)[12]

From these two quotes, the recent pressures for improved planning and performance management from a Citizen-Government perspective are highlighted next:

- Maximum input and feedback for decision making.
- Recognition of the impact that Local Government can have.
- The need for efficiency and effectiveness.
- Public accountability and transparency.
- Public pressure and the need to improve public trust
- Increased demands for citizen participation.

From a Cross-Governmental perspective there are also pressures for:

- Feedback into funding allocation decisions.
- Feedback into program design decisions.
- Comparison and benchmarking purposes.
- Accountability needs.
- Audit needs to program rule and guidelines.
- Input into program evaluation.

However, there is a recognized need for strategic and performance management from an internal-organizational

---

12   Independent Pricing and Regulatory Tribunal (IPART), Benchmarking Local Government Performance in New South Wales – An Issues Paper, NSW Government, Australia, 1997

perspective. Simply, this means that performance information is not only accurately collected, but also the results are used as part of an integrated system of management. Whether or not there may be any external pressures, many government authorities are developing their strategies and performance management systems to meet their own organizational needs.

The history of planning in the corporate arena progressed significantly in the past few years and with it the needed technological tools. As companies have sought to better allocate resources and bring predictability to their financial performance, the processes and technologies of business planning have continually evolved together over time. Before the introduction of computers, companies performed planning tasks with paper spreadsheets and calculators. This "technology" required documents to be physically sent between locations, and didn't provide any way to automatically link values from one document to another. Planning as a completely manual process was slow, prone to error, and extremely inflexible. The introduction of PCs and desktop spreadsheets quickly revolutionized the way organizations planned and managed their strategic plans and budgets. While desktop spreadsheets were not true planning tools, business users could create planning documents in a digital format that could be easily shared and updated, and which contained much more information and detail.

Responding to their growing use in planning and budgeting processes, technology vendors next began enhancing the basic spreadsheet with specialized planning and budgeting applications. These tools provided embedded capabilities to handle compound growth rates, currency variables and other factors that were beyond the functionality offered by a standard, un-enhanced spreadsheet application. These enhancements enabled businesses to more quickly and consistently build planning documents based on more sophisticated and more accurate models of the business operations. They also enabled more unified planning across multiple lines of the business. However, these calculation-related enhancements did not address fundamental issues of process management, auditing and the linkage of planning documents to key enterprise data sources.

Another wave of technological change came to planning with the introduction of the Internet. Now, instead of having a "fat client" application distributed across the enterprise, companies could provide browser-based access to shared planning databases and documents. These documents could thus be maintained on a central web server, rather than being dispersed across multiple users' desktops. This Web-enabled architecture provided significant process advantages over its desktop predecessors. With documents maintained in a central location, version control and auditing could be introduced into the planning process. Because these documents were now stationary, budget values could be automatically populated with data from other documents and systems, and triggers could be set to automatically notify managers about variances. However, these management and integration capabilities remained limited, and planning remained largely a static, top-down process, rather than a dynamic process, and tightly linked to core business applications.[13]

This shows that advances in corporate planning practices are largely contingent upon advances in planning technology. Each stage of technological advance has yielded important enhancements in how business users collaborate to optimize

13   Enterprise Planning: Linking Strategies, Plans And Resources For Competitive Advantage, 6/27/1905, Hyperion

the planning process and the allocation of corporate resources. For this reason, any progress in this arena has to address both planning process and the utilizing of related technology.

1.2 Today's Issues and Challenges

Over the past few decades, many new strategic management methods were introduced to help organizations improve their performance and competitive advantage in the market place. Unfortunately, the majority of these organizations still fail to implement and manage their strategies. This book contributes to the body of knowledge in solving this long-lived myth.

According to a recent survey done by Palladium Group, 70% to 90% of organizations fail to successfully execute their strategies. In most cases, the failure is blamed on strategy execution, not on strategy development. Studying planning disciplines and management tools presents a challenge. When it comes to strategic management, with success rates of only 10% to 30%, there is no shortage of failures cases to study. Even though failure is more visible and easier to describe, this book focus on studying few success factors as well that involves doing things well. [14]

According to Eric Beinhocker and Dr. Kaplan, "many companies get little value from their annual strategic planning process. It should be redesigned to support real-time strategy making and to encourage 'creative accidents.'"[15] Typical strategy management in most organizations includes some combination of the following activities:

- Strategy is updated in a strategic retreat.
- Divisions and support units develop their own plans using their own processes. They create their own mission and vision statements, and they decide how, and whether to, be aligned with the corporate strategy.

---

14   Dr. Robert Kaplan & David Norton, Strategic Management - An Emerging Profession, 1/25/2004, Balanced Scorecard Collaborative, pp. 1-4
15   Eric Beinhocker & Sarah Kaplan, Tired of Strategic Planning, 2002 Number 2, The McKinsey Quarterly, pp. 1-7

- Later in the year, Finance coordinates the budget compilation that authorizes next year's spending on operations, discretionary programs, capital investments, and establishes next year's targets for key financial metrics.
- Late in the year, HR runs the annual performance review process, determines bonus and compensation decisions, and asks employees to update their objectives for the following year.
- Throughout the next year, executives meet monthly or quarterly to review progress against the budget and initiate actions to meet short-term performance issues.

This group of activities is rarely connected and coordinated, and often results in confusion and misalignment. In turn, as results of typical strategy management are generally negative and do not support achievement of strategy. Dr. Robert Kaplan stated during a 2008 conference, that most organizations have problem executing their strategy. He supported this view by listing the following sources.[16]

- "Less than 10% of strategies effectively formulated are effectively executed." Fortune Magazine
- "Only 15% of the 794 programs reviewed in Fiscal 2005 were rated effective" Barron's
- "Our problem is not about the strategy itself but about our execution of it" Tony Hayward, CEO, BP
- "I'd rather have a mediocre strategy that is well executed than a brilliant strategy executed poorly" Jamie Dimon CEO, J.P. Morgan Chase

Today, building a strategy is one of the most important activities on senior executives' agendas. In turn, many organizations invest a lot of time and effort in a structured strategic-planning process that typically initiates many reviews and meetings

---

16   Dr. Robert Kaplin, - 2008 BSC Form

between operational business units and top management team. Despite this effort and resources, few executives think this time-consuming and long process pays off, and many top managers complain that their strategic-planning process yields few new ideas and it is in most cases loaded with politics and hidden agendas.[17]

This belief led many to question why this gap exists between effort and result. Studies that was collected from research on the planning processes indicates a frequent and disappointing explanation: on-going strategy review produce little more than an opportunity where business unit and division managers present similar updates usually taken from last year's presentations, take little risks by not giving new and drastic ideas, and make sure to keep away from embarrassing facts and figures. In other words, the planning process becomes a show.[18]

In a desirable environment, business unit and division managers are asked to prepare top managers to face and mitigate potential risk in the future and to support creative thinking about a company's vision and direction. Instead, in many cases, managers are not exactly sure why they do strategic planning, but there is a strong hope that something positive will come out of it. In a business environment of high risk and uncertainty, developing effective strategies is crucial. The challenge becomes how organizations reform the strategic planning process in order to get the benefit and outcomes that they require.[19]

In recent years, in public sector, there has also been a worldwide interest in the models of so-called "New Managerialism" and "New Public Sector Management". These models are based on

---

17   Keith Hammonds, You've got to make time for strategy, 3/1/2001, Illustrations, pp. 1-6
18   Henry Mintzberg, The Pitfalls Of Strategic Planning, Fall, 1993, California Management Review
19   Eric Beinhocker & Sarah Kaplan, Tired of Strategic Planning, 2002 Number 2, The McKinsey Quarterly, pp. 1-7

a fundamental concept that public sector organizations can borrow many of the management strategies from the private sector. One such fundamental strategy is that the organization must measure and evaluate its performance in order to minimize waste and maximize output. Strategic planning and performance management are at the heart of many current management paradigms such as Total Quality Management (TQM) and can even lead to practices such as Activity Based Costing (ABC) and Activity Based Management (ABM).

Osborne and Gaebler, in their important book "Reinventing Government" outlined a number of key incentives for performance management in "new" public sector organizations:[20]

- What gets measured gets done.
- If management doesn't measure results, management can't tell success from failure.
- If management can't see success management can't reward it.
- If management can't see success, management can't learn from it.
- If management can't reward success, management is probably rewarding failure.
- If management can't recognize failure, management can't correct it.
- If management demonstrates results, management can win public support.

From all of these perspectives; government-citizen; inter-governmental; and inter-organizational; it is clear that there is a growing pressure for both improved planning and performance management. Current common *weaknesses* could be organized into two broad categories:

---

20   Osborne, D. & Gaebler, R., Reinventing Government, 1992

Common *weaknesses* in planning and management of public services:

- ✗ Effectiveness and efficiency of the services are not being measured enough.
- ✗ Information is not being used to help improve the delivery of services.
- ✗ Management decisions are not well- informed and well-planned enough.
- ✗ Limited resources are not well-used and wastage exists.

Common *weaknesses* in accountability and citizen participation:

- ✗ Measurements are not accurately reported.
- ✗ Results are not made available for public view.
- ✗ Citizens are not involved in setting objectives and performance indicators.

Many initiatives have been launched by international bodies that have focused particularly on performance management in local government. For example:

- A Brief Guide for Performance Measurement in Local Government. National Center for Public Productivity, Rutgers University.
- The Western Australian Department of Local Government and Performance Management for Local Government. This publication seeks to provide brief and simple guidelines that can assist any local government to start performance management.
- The United Kingdom Audit Commission.

Most of these initiatives have focused on a performance auditing role. In other words, they have been imposed on government agencies and have often been tied to funding agreements with higher levels of government. There has been a perception among government authorities, that such comparisons are used to grant either benefits or punishments depending on the achieved results.

In addition, many of the so called "Public Sector Reform" developments across the world have also introduced regimes that have a strong element of performance management. Many countries have introduced market competition into areas of government services, with some countries (i.e. United Kingdom, New Zealand, Australia) introducing Compulsory Competitive Tendering (CCT). By forcing government agencies to compete with private sector providers, such government regimes essentially hold on to the belief that they are measuring the performance of a public sector institution against the performance of a private sector company. The "New Managerialism" movement of the 1980s and 1990s has seen the introduction of government policies across the world that have perhaps the most disciplinary of performance management regimes. In short, the message was if a government agency performance cannot beat the private sector, particularly on cost, then it will lose funding and support.

Further, the United Kingdom government has developed a significantly different approach that recognizes the value of decisions about government performance. Under the "Best Value" program, local authorities are expected to discuss, negotiate and engage with their communities to jointly develop levels of "Best Value" like agreed statements of performance that are expected in the local community and which recognize local circumstances. Recent developments have also focused around the concepts of "Public Value" and have encouraged local government to develop "Quality of life indicators" with their own communities. This is a significant development in the United Kingdom system that truly respects local governance. This important element of involving the community in developing goals, targets and indicators will be an important issue for the future.[21]

21   Robert Mellor, Performance Measurement & Management In Asian-Pacific Local Government, 9/1/2003, The Network of Local Government Training and Research, pp. 2-69

1.3 Focus and Objective

To be able to implement the strategic plan successfully, *weaknesses* have to be addressed and fixed at multiple stages of the process. This book explores the strategic planning cycle, and it has two objectives. First, to clarify why some organizations effectively implement their strategic plans while many others fail to do so. Second, to understand what are the most effective tools used to successfully implement a strategic plan.

Most organization management (including government and non-profit agencies) without an effective strategic plan spend most of their time reacting to unexpected changes instead of anticipating and preparing for them. These organizations, are usually caught off guard, may spend a great deal of time, money, and energy playing catch up. They use up their resources addressing day-to-day and operational problems with little time and effort left to forecast and prepare for the next challenges. This common situation keeps many organizations into a reactive mode instead being in a proactive mode.

Having a strategic plan is not enough by itself. Each organization has to have step by step planning process with clear goals and priorities that can be implemented, measured, and evaluated later on. This area is where the challenge exists in most cases, and where the benefit of having a strategic plan is not fully realized. Likewise, the wide range of popular writings related to performance management is common to find; this book will address the proven performance methods and most used ones.

CHAPTER 2

STRATEGIC PLAN DEVELOPMENT

CHAPTER 2: STRATEGIC PLAN DEVELOPMENT

Strategic planning is a long-term, future-oriented process of assessment, goal setting, and strategy building that maps a path between the present and a vision of the future, that relies on careful consideration of an organization's capabilities and environment, and leads to priority-based resource allocation and other decisions. [22]

The management cycle begins with the company's strategic plan. This usually takes place at an annual offsite meeting during which the management team either improves an existing strategic plan or introduces an entirely new one. Strategic plan generally have three to five years of useful life. In this chapter, strategic plan development process will be covered including; effective methods used to develop strategic plans.

Private and public organizations find themselves continually trying to do more with less. Stephen Covey said once: "People and their managers are working so hard to be sure things are done right, that they hardly have time to decide if they are doing the right things." Doing the right things and doing things right is a balancing act, and requires the development of good strategic plans. Competitive pressures on private businesses and public sector organizations mandate that organizations continually worry about developing good strategic plans, at the same time they worry about running business operations efficiently. Today's organizations need to be both strategically and operationally excellent to survive and meet tomorrow's challenges.[23]

22   Dept. of Finance, Strategic Planning Guidelines - California State, 3/1/1998, California State Government, pp. 6-44
23   Howard Rohm, A Balancing Act, Vol 2 Issue 2, Reform Magazine, pp. 1-8

Dr. Jan Rivkin from Harvard Business School identified strategy as: "an integrated set of choices that position a firm, in an industry, to earn superior returns over the long run." He stated that three tests of a good strategy can be defined: [24]

- *External Consistency*: Where the strategy capitalizes on the opportunities and neutralizes the threats in a unique way.
- *Internal Consistency*: Strategy parts fit together so the whole is the greater that the sum of the parts.
- *Dynamic Consistency*: Where the strategy call on the firm to do today the things it needs to do tomorrow to be successful. The strategy accurately anticipates competitive responses and handles these before they become problems.

Dr. Mintzberg stated that "Strategy" tends to be defined narrowly in practice and is typically associated with a plan or a series of steps or actions designed to move an organization from its current state to a future one. While these definitions are accurate, they represent only one dimension of strategy. Strategy can mean many different things depending upon how it is used. [25]

In a book titled "Strategy Safari: A Guided Tour Through the Wilds of Strategic Management", Henry Mintzberg, Bruce Ahlstrand and Joseph Lampel discuss ten different schools of strategy. While the authors acknowledge that some of the schools are really more concepts than firm constructs, they do illustrate in the book how each school provides a useful lens to examine the ways in which organizations think about and create strategy. The authors describe the ten schools in the following list:

---

24   Jan Rivkin, "Where do great strategies come from?" Harvard Business School Faculty Seminar Series Lecture

25   Henry Mintzberg, Bruce Ahlstrand and Joseph Lampel. Strategy Safari: A guided tour through the wilds of strategic management, 1998, Free Press, New York

- *Design School*: Strategy formation is a process of conception and individuals, if not management teams, can architect strategy.
- *Planning School*: Strategy formation is formal process that typically results in the generation of a plan.
- *Positioning School*: Strategy formation is an analytical process that positions a firm within a market.
- *Entrepreneurial School*: Strategy formation is a visionary process that is most often associated with a firm founder.
- *Cognitive School*: Strategy formation is a mental process that is heavily dependent upon the mental maps for frames of reference managers use.
- *Learning School*: Strategy formation is an emergent process that emphasizes experience and adaptation.
- *Power School*: Strategy formation is a process of negotiation where strategy is influenced heavily by those possessing power and key relationships within an organization.
- *Cultural School*: Strategy formation is a collective process where the strategy selected is largely dependent upon the beliefs and values of the firm.
- *Environmental School*: Strategy formation is a reactive process where the strategy is determined by the conditions in the environment and the firm's responses to those conditions.
- *Configuration School*: Strategy formation is process of transformation where the firm periodically reconfigures in response to internal or external stimuli.

The strategy development process requires the formation and operation of strategy team. This team includes core, leadership, and analytics team members. This team conducts executive workshops that will get top management to buy-in into the strategy.

Core team members are responsible for driving the strategy development process from start to finish. They help collect and analyze the initial data that will be needed to successfully inform the process.

Leadership team-members provide leadership, endorsement, and vision for the strategy. They are the ultimate owners of the strategy so they must provide a clear vision and destination for the organization as well as actually set the strategy. They also ensure that their strategy is reflected in the execution and consistent with Board of Directors expectations.

Analytics team-members provide detailed, on demand analysis of relevant external and internal variables needed to inform the strategy development process. Better data and information lead to better quality decision-making and ultimately, outcomes.

Pioneering strategy thinkers like Chester Barnard (The Functions of The Executive, 1938), Alfred Chandler (Strategy and Structure, 1962), and Ken Andrews (The Concept of Corporate Strategy, 1971) have always emphasized the strong relationship between developing and implementing strategy. For many years however, emphasis in both practice and publication has been placed on the design of strategy versus the implementation of strategy. Tools like the Balanced Scorecard and similar performance management frameworks (i.e. EVA) have shifted thinking more recently to improving the quality of execution. In practice it seems that organizations tend to build competencies in one dimension of Strategy Management at the expense of the others. In reality neither a great plan poorly executed, nor a poor plan well executed is of much value.

Organizations are somewhat unclear about how they go about selecting techniques to develop their strategies. Some managers rely on what their consultants say. Others default to methods they have successfully applied in the past. The key to success is selecting the right tool for the job. The strategy tool selected by the organization needs to be consistent with the targeted customer segments to be served. The following are strategy development techniques that are used by many industries today:

- *Activity-Based Costing* and *Time Driven Activity Based Costing* are techniques that allocate financial data to activities and processes in order to accurately assess the costs of individual products, services and customers.
- *Blue Ocean Strategy* seeks to innovate and create new value for customers (Blue Ocean) while at the same time reducing or eliminating costly activities or features that fail to do so.
- *Experience Co-Creation* is a technique that seeks to understand the interactions an organization has with its customers as a means of understanding and improving where and how value is exchanged.
- *Profit from-the-Core* is a technique that uses adjacency mapping to identify opportunities in new business growth opportunities that are most closely related to the 'core' business.
- *Open Innovation* notes that knowledge today is widely distributed and that the best R&D ideas cannot be generated exclusively by an organization's in-house capabilities.
- *Judo Strategy* takes advantage of speed, flexibility and leverage to beat competitors. It is based upon resource and capability configurations of competitors.

The essential starting point for formation of the strategy is the strategy gap. The strategy gap is the quantifiable difference between where the organization is currently and its desired future state. Without determining the magnitude of the strategy gap, it is difficult to understand the sources and extent of improvement required in future performance. The strategy gap can be expressed in many different terms, such as; shareholder value; market share; revenue growth; profit improvement; cost reduction; or improvement of performance. Common *weaknesses* exist at strategy development stage; examples of these *weaknesses* are described below:

- ✗ Not sure what skills does the organization need internally (i.e. workforce talents). to enable the execution of strategy.
- ✗ Strategy total cost is not clear, unknown strategy cost to implement.
- ✗ No senior management adequately secured buy-in.
- ✗ Not enough testing and understanding of the current situation.
- ✗ Measures and KPIs were not properly defined.
- ✗ The fear of change and of the unknown or unexplored situations.
- ✗ Selecting and funding the wrong strategic initiatives.
- ✗ Lock out strategy team and withhold information.
- ✗ Not adequate framework for developing strategy.
- ✗ The strategy development process not effective.
- ✗ Transparency and openness identified as a restrictive issue.
- ✗ Not determining the magnitude of the strategy gap.
- ✗ Not obvious what and how the organization can serve its customers.
- ✗ Not clear which customers the organization will serve and where.

The important and critical items for strategy development check list are designed to address the content, process, and impact of the strategic plan during the development phase. The following are the recommended *check list* items:

- ✓ The strategy followed on from a well-articulated and relevant vision.

- ✓ The vision been translated into a set of clear objectives.
- ✓ The strategy development sufficiently addresses the internal and external strategic challenges facing the organization.
- ✓ Strong correlation between the vision, mission, values and the strategy.
- ✓ Senior leadership motivating the organization towards the development of corporate strategy.
- ✓ Provide organizational support by establishing dedicated strategic planning unit for the organization.
- ✓ The need for change being made clear.
- ✓ The strategy well understood by the organization.
- ✓ All employees are clear on how they will contribute to it.
- ✓ Adequate buy-in from all areas of the organization.
- ✓ Objectives adequately cover the goals, for which the organization is expected to operate.
- ✓ Organization goals are properly communicated to help develop business unit's strategic objectives.
- ✓ Organization's objectives been sufficiently broken down into specific sub-objectives and targets that represent the aims of the strategic objectives.
- ✓ The strategy been articulated into a form that can be easily communicated.
- ✓ Clear and unambiguous relationships between expected goals and strategic objectives; objectives and other objectives through cause-effect links; objectives and measures/initiatives.
- ✓ Used tools, components, and processes (i.e. SWOT Analysis) of developing strategy been applied consistently across organization.
- ✓ Various elements of the strategy developed produce the strategy needed to raise the performance of the organization.
- ✓ Using strategy framework not too elaborate and too complex.

✓ Need for change made clear. The 'why' needs to receive significant focus in communication messages.

✓ Use of bottom-up along with top-down strategy and spend more effort on the middle connection to ensure smooth cascading.

✓ Leveraging a formal strategy analysis framework.

✓ Improve employee clarity on how to contribute to strategy.

✓ Selecting the proper initiatives to be funded.

✓ Doing sufficient analysis on proposed initiatives, which requires adequate time and experience in the nature of the project.

✓ Organizations set clearly their list of priorities for funding.

✓ Enhanced budgeting system to support strategy development process.

✓ Strategy map supported by strategy management system.

2.1 Vision, Mission, and Values

Before formulating a strategic plan, managers need to agree on their company's aspiration for future results (vision), its purpose (mission), and the internal compass that will guide its actions (values).[26]

In a research conducted by Schiemann & Associates Inc. to understand agreement on strategy, only 7 percent of measurement-managed companies reported a lack of agreement among top management on the business strategy of the organization. This compared to 63 percent of the non-measurement-managed organizations. The act of translating vision or strategy into measurable objectives forces specificity. It helps to surface and resolve those hidden disagreements that often get buried when the strategy remains vague, only to return at some later date to haunt an organization.[27]

Perhaps the most important responsibility senior managers have within their organization is direction setting. Vision, mission and values should provide guidance to the board of directors, business partners, customers and employees regarding the organization's direction. In the absence of this vital information, direction of the organization will be unclear and could contribute to a misuse of valuable resources (i.e. time and money) in pursuit of a strategy that is not aligned with the true course of the organization.

The vision is a concise statement that defines the mid- to long-term (3 to 10-year) goals of the organization. The vision should focus on the picture instead of the statement, can be reached although not easily, and should be both inspirational and

---

26   Dr. Robert Kaplan & David Norton, Mastering the Management System, 1/1/2008, Harvard Business Review, pp. 3-17

27   John H. Lingle, From BSC to IS Measurement, 1/1/2007, Wm. Schiemann & Associates Inc, pp. 1-6

aspirational. The vision should address where the organization is going and what the future looks like. Common *weaknesses* in developing vision statement are summarized next:[28]

- ✗ Does not presents where the organization wants to go.
- ✗ Not easy to read and understand.
- ✗ Does not capture the desired spirit of an organization.
- ✗ Is not compact and can not be used to guide decision-making.
- ✗ Does not get people's attention.
- ✗ Does not describe a preferred and meaningful future state.
- ✗ Does not gives people good understanding of how their individual purpose could be realized in the group.
- ✗ Does not provide a motivating force.
- ✗ Is not challenging and compelling, and not stretching the organization beyond what is comfortable.

The mission is a brief statement, typically one or two sentences, that defines why the organization exists, especially what it offers to its customers and clients. An effective mission statement addresses the following points:

- ✓ Broad description of what the organization does.
- ✓ With and for whom the organization does it.
- ✓ The organization distinctive competence. (How the organization does it "differently", "better", "more effectively" than others)
- ✓ Why the organization does it (Its ultimate end reason)

Common *weaknesses* in developing mission statement are described below:[29]

---

28   Frank Martinelli, Strategic Planning in Nonprofit and Public Sector Organizations, 1/1/1999, The Center for Public Skills Training, pp. 28-35
29   Dr. Robert Kaplan & David Norton, Mastering the Management System, 1/1/2008, Harvard Business Review, pp. 3-17

- ✘ Is not clear or/and using vague language.
- ✘ Is not on target in today's operating environment.
- ✘ Does not address what the organization does.
- ✘ Does not state the organization end customer.
- ✘ Does not list the organization distinctive competence.
- ✘ Duplicate the vision of the organization.

Values deals with what the organization believe in and what it stands for. It is specific and meaningful to the organization. It doesn't have to be politically correct necessarily but most are today. Values and statements of values have historically focused internally on what the organization believes itself to be. Today, more and more organizations are adopting statements of ethics and codes of conduct that extend beyond the simple listing of internal organizational beliefs and state their views on the stakeholder environments to include communities in which they operate, customers affected and suppliers they partner with. Corporate Social Responsibility (CSR) is being reflected more frequently in value statements regarding what organizations believe in, mainly because it is just good business.

Values audit provides a way to understand, ideally at the start of a planning process, how well employees believe the organization is living its values. Some organizations will not conduct values audits or reviews because they may be concerned with what they might find out. It is difficult to improve workforce competitiveness without an accurate assessment of true workforce beliefs.

2.2 Environmental Scanning

Organizations don't exist by themselves. They exist in complex systems comprised of their internal and external environments. For this reason, organizations are constantly in shift as they change internally to keep pace with their environments. Organizations that can change internally to adapt with external changes are said to be properly positioned into their environment. The most common elements of an organization's external environment are customers, suppliers, partners, competitors, political, regulatory institutions, economic conditions, and technology. It is useful to think of these in macro and micro terms.[30]

Critics of the environmental scanning process state that all scanning does, is spending a great deal of time collecting data that is irrelevant or already known. When scanning does uncover important information, it supposed to be used to influence decisions. Doing something badly doesn't mean it shouldn't be done to begin with; it should be done correctly to provide benefits. An important step in making scanning useful is to focus the effort. Identify from the levels and elements where the organization's key efforts should be directed. It is a good idea to solicit input and support from senior managers to ensure that time used in the environmental scanning process is used effectively.

Environmental scanning is a methodology that may be difficult to observe or diagnose but that cannot be ignored and will not go away. In summary, environmental scanning:[31]

- Is important to aid in framing strategy development activities.
- Can be done to various depths and at various levels.

---

30   Palladium BSC Master Class Handbook 2008
31   Stoffels, J. Strategic Issues Management: A Comprehensive Guide to Environmental Scanning, Pergamon, 1994, pp. 1.

- Ideally should be issues-based to avoid wasting time and energy.
- Effectiveness is dependent upon choosing the right tool for the job.
- Can provide the context for scenario development.

In order to conduct an effective environmental scan three steps should be followed. While the depth and extent of each sub-step will vary by organization (due to capabilities and resources) the primary three main steps are addressed in the following three paragraphs.

The first step in environmental scanning requires identifying a scanning strategy, selecting scanning framework and collecting data. Managers are challenged by the fact that scanning can become an endless exercise given the nature of information today. To focus the scanning effort, it is essential to identify what the organization wants to know up front. For example, what are the most important trends facing the organization, or what are the most critical activities the organization performs in meeting its customer's expectations.

The second step in conducting an effective scan requires synthesizing information collected during the scan and evaluating key issues that will likely affect the organization. There is no one right way to synthesize and summarize data. Some organizations prefer a comprehensive written report. Others like the ease of use associated with slide presentations. Regardless of how organizations do environmental scanning, it is critical that the scan is complete in that it should address scanning goals. It is consistent so that the data fit together. It is easy to use so it can be referenced prior to starting development.

The final step requires communication of the findings to the users of the information to help update decision-makers. The purpose of scanning is to inform the development process.

Therefore, the results must be communicated, socialized and discussed to be understood. This may be the most important step in conducting the scan. For this reason, it is important to allocate plenty of time to it. It is possible that the results of the scan may change some of the original assumptions associated with the initial direction setting.

Environmental scanning can cover many areas outside and inside an organization. Many tools are currently used to do environmental scanning such as:

- *Porter's Five Forces* framework is a micro tool for examining the industry in which an organization competes. (bargaining power of buyers; bargaining power of suppliers; availability of substitutes; threat of new entrants; and industry rivalry)
- *PESTEL* analysis is a macro level tool used to examine the broader external environment. (Political, Economic, Social, Technological, Environmental, and Legal factors)
- *The Value Chain* represents the sequence and configuration of business activities that deliver value to customers.
- *SWOT* analysis is mostly used by organizations to know their Strengths, Weaknesses, Opportunities, and Threats.

Top managers must know the key issues their organization is facing. In turn, they have to undertake a strategic analysis of the organization's micro and macro external situation.

For the micro part, management team studies the industry's using frameworks such as *Michael Porter's Five Forces Model*. Developed in the late 1970's, Harvard Business School Professor Michael Porter's Five Forces Model is a mainstay within the area of competitive strategy. This micro analysis cover areas related to bargaining power of buyers; bargaining power of suppliers;

availability of substitutes; threat of new entrants; and industry rivalry issues. There are a few things to keep in mind when using Porter's Five Forces model:

- The organization can conduct analysis from the standpoint of firms within the industry. Given the analysis is intended to gauge industry attractiveness; the perspective that must be taken is from inside the industry.
- The organization should look for the forces that have the most impact. Some forces are more influential than others.
- The organization should not use the model in isolation; instead it should be used in conjunction with other analyses. The Five Forces is a very useful analysis but its value is greatly enhanced when it is applied in conjunction with other analysis such as industry-wide ratio analysis or profit analysis or competitive benchmarking within the industry.

For the macro part, the team assesses the external macro environment using frameworks such as *PESTEL* framework. This macro analysis cover areas related to political, economic, social, technological, environmental, and legal issues:

- Political: covers the regulatory issues, forms of legislation that could affect the organization.
- Economic: covers major trends in the economy such as oil prices, interest rates, reduction in income or real spending exist.
- Social: covers major changes in tastes, preferences and behaviors.
- Technological: covers significant developments on the technology frontier that could impact the organization.
- Environmental: covers environmental concerns that could face the business.

- Legal: covers prevailing legal conditions and how they might affect business dealings.

After the external analysis is done, managers should assess the company's internal capabilities and performance. One tool widely used is *Value Chain Model*. Initially developed by McKinsey and then advanced by Porter, it represents the sequence and configuration of business activities that deliver value to customers. Value Chain Model has the following *strengths*:

- ✓ It categorizes capabilities used in the processes of developing, producing, delivering, and selling products or services to customers.
- ✓ Internal analysis could identify the distinctive resources and capabilities that give the firm its competitive advantage in the market place.
- ✓ The primary way a generic strategy is evaluated is through analysis of an organization's value chain.
- ✓ It is considered one of the most important tools in all of strategy analysis because it enables both development and detailed cost analysis.

The Economist Intelligence Unit (EIU) surveyed 154 global executives (the survey was commissioned by Business Objects) and found the following results:[32]

- Less than 1% of executives believe they have the information necessary to make critical business decisions.
- More than 25% believe that management frequently or always makes the wrong decisions.
- More than 50% said decision-making is mostly informal or ad hoc.
- 80% believe data is more important than intuition.

---

32   The Economist Intelligence Unit (EIU) / Business Objects, 2007

Correctly identifying key issues is a critical step to target strategy development activities. Without focus on the critical few challenges facing an organization, great effort can be expended analyzing issues that have little impact. Pinpointing the list of strategic issues enables more effective and efficient strategy development. There are two basic approaches to structuring thinking inside the strategy development process: deductive and inductive reasoning: [33]

- In deductive reasoning, evidence (i.e. data) is gathered, facts are identified and conclusions are drawn. Using deduction, conclusions are drawn only as they relate to the specific evidence gathered.
- During induction, evidence is gathered, facts are identified; however, generalizations rather than conclusions are made about a context broader than those simply represented by the initial evidence.

Organizations are improving their analytical capabilities. This maturity model provided by Professor Tom Davenport and researcher Jeanne Harris of Babson College shows the path of progress. In their book "Competing on analytics: The New Science of Winning", Tom Davenport and Jeanne Harris profile a variety of analytical applications for both internal and external processes. Here is a sampling of those that apply to internal processes:[34]

- *Bayesian Inference*: A numerical estimate of the degree of belief in a hypothesis before and after the evidence has been observed. (used to predict revenues)
- *Constraint Analysis*: The use of one or more constraint satisfaction algorithms to specify the set of feasible solutions. Constraints are programmed in rules or

---

33   Barbara Minto, The Pyramid Principle, by Financial Times, 2002
34   Davenport, T and Harris, J., Competing on analytics: The New Science of Winning, Harvard Business School Press, 2007

procedures that produce solutions to particular configurations and design problems using one or more constraint satisfaction algorithms. (used for product configuration).

- *Future-Value Analysis*: The decomposition of market capitalization into current value (extrapolation of existing monetary value) and future value or expectations of future growth.

- *Monte Carlo Simulation*: A computerized technique used to asses the probability of certain outcomes or risks by mathematically modeling a hypothesis event over multiple trials and comparing the outcome with predefined probability distributions. (used for R&D project valuation)

- *Yield Analysis*: Employing basic statistics (mean, median, standard deviation) to understand yield volume, quality and to compare one batch of items with another. Often displayed visually. (used in semiconductor manufacturing)

- *Multiple Regression Analysis*: A statistical technique whereby the influence of a set of independent variables on a single dependent variable is determined. (used to determine how non-financial factors affect financial performance)

- *Textual Analysis*: Analysis of the frequency, semantic relationships, and relative importance of particular terms, phrases and documents in online texts. (used to assess intangible capabilities)

Finally, management summarizes the conclusions from the external and internal analyses in a *SWOT* matrix, the main goal here is to ensure that the strategy uses internal strengths to capture external opportunities, while limiting weaknesses and threats. SWOT matrix has the following *strengths*: [35]

---

35   Dr. Robert Kaplan & David Norton, Mastering the Management System, 1/1/2008, Harvard Business Review, pp. 3-17

- ✓ Assess the ability of internal capacity in relation to external factors.
- ✓ One of the most widely used and basic tools in strategy development.
- ✓ Match internal firm capabilities (strengths and weaknesses) with external environment (opportunities and threats).
- ✓ Can be improved by adding additional levels of analysis.
- ✓ Can be used to weight issues by adding positive or negative values.
- ✓ An effective way to prioritize key issues that affect strategy development.

2.3 Strategic Goals and Objectives

Strategic goals are derived from the vision and mission of the organization but describe, more precisely, what is to be achieved. Objectives describe the desired end result from achieving strategic goals. Goals and objectives are important because they help to structure the translation of the vision and mission into organization priorities.

Translating strategy to operation requires clarity and specifics. Defining strategic objectives keeps the record of what executives have committed the organization to achieving. Generic objective definitions could be damaging because they reduce the ability to implement the strategy due to build-in vagueness. This definition exercise can typically be accomplished in three to five sentences for each objective. [36]

Objectives are a powerful way to make strategy actionable. They provide an organization with specific targets, which when combined, support achievement of the organization's strategy. In other words, objectives are action statements that clarify how the organization will implement the strategy. A good set of objectives should possess the following characteristics:

    ✓   Reflect systems and logical thinking.
    ✓   Be actionable and begin with a verb.
    ✓   Be inspirational.
    ✓   Be appropriately achievable.

Common *weaknesses* that organizations encounter when setting strategic objectives are listed below:

    ✖   Too many objectives that could cause loss of focus or be too tactical.

---

36   Andrew J. Pateman,, Five easy steps for developing your BSC measures, 4/1/2004, Balanced Scorecard Report, pp. 15-17

- ✖ Objectives are mostly financial-related that produce unbalanced strategy.
- ✖ Objectives are not aligned or mutually achievable.
- ✖ Objectives are not actionable within the organization.
- ✖ Objectives aggregate multiple concepts (i.e. recruit and develop workforce).
- ✖ Lack of agreement in developing objectives.

Fuzzy strategic objective is a common issue that has to be addressed at early stage. "If you wish to debate with me, define your terms." Aristotle's advice is equally valid for managing organizations. It's tough to run a business without clearly defined objectives. The development of solid strategic plan requires that goals and objectives be defined with sufficient precision to be measurable later on. Typically, this precision exists in the financial and operational areas. According to a research conducted by W. Schiemann & Associates Inc, many companies do not invest the time needed to define with equal precision other areas of performance, such as customer satisfaction, employee performance and rate of change. A first step in achieving precision in hard to quantify areas is to translate vague objectives into clear statements of results and then determine how the result can be measured.[37]

Strategy Map illustrates how internal objectives of the strategy are linked to the customer, financial, or stakeholder objectives. The strategy map ensures that the key outcomes and drivers of value remain at the center of what gets managed. The strategy map provides a context to organize measures. A properly constructed map contains strategic objectives. Executives must be very clear about the intent of each objective. Skipping this

---

[37]   John H. Lingle, From BSC to IS Measurement, 1/1/2007, Wm. Schiemann & Associates Inc, pp. 1-6

step could cause management team to struggles to stay on course.[38]

Scenario Planning is recommended before setting strategic goals and objectives. Scenario Planning is a disciplined method for imagining possible alternate futures. Scenarios try to capture new states that will develop after major shocks or deviations in key variables.

Scenario planning is a futures technique used for medium to long-term strategic analysis and planning. It is used to develop policies and strategies that are robust, resilient, flexible, and innovative. Scenarios are stories set in the future, which describe how the world might look in, say 2020. They explore how the world would change if certain trends were to strengthen or diminish, or various events were to occur. Normally a set of scenarios are developed (between two and five) representing different possible futures, associated with different trends and events.

These scenarios are then used to review or test a range of plans and policy options. The conclusion generally being that different plans are likely to work better in different scenarios. Alternatively scenarios can be used to stimulate the development of new strategy. They are also a useful means of identifying 'early warning' indicators that signal a shift towards a certain kind of future. At any given point in time, there are an infinite number of possible future scenarios. Scenario planning does not attempt to predict which of these will occur, but through a formal development process identifies a limited set of examples of possible futures that provide a valuable point of reference when evaluating current strategies or developing new ones.[39]

---

38   Andrew J. Pateman,, Five easy steps for developing your BSC measures, 4/1/2004, Balanced Scorecard Report, pp. 15-17
39   Foresight Horizon Scanning 2009

They identify patterns and clusters among several possible outcomes and often include elements that cannot be formally modeled, such as new regulations or innovations. Hence, scenario planning goes beyond objective and goals analyses and tends to include subjective interpretations. It is used in strategic planning and most effective when there is high uncertainty in the external environment, or there have been too many costly surprises in the past, or the quality of strategic planning is low.

Scenario planning attempts to compensate for two common errors in decision-making, under prediction and over prediction of change, by charting a middle ground between both whereby the range of possibilities that can be seen increases without drifting into pure science fiction. Scenario planning does this by dividing knowledge into:

- Things we can be almost certain about (i.e. demographic shifts, substitution effects of new technology)
- Elements we consider uncertain or unknowable (i.e. future interest rates, oil prices, political election results)

Scenario planning is usually conducted through common process. It is not important to account for all the possible outcomes of each uncertainty; simplifying the possible outcomes is sufficient for scenario planning (i.e. consider three interest rate levels – high, medium, low rather than hundreds that might be possible). The purpose is not to cover all possibilities but to confine them. The process for developing scenarios includes:[40]

- *Defining the Scope*: Set the time frame and scope of analysis (in terms of services, geographies and technologies) and ask what knowledge would be of greatest value that far down the road.

---

40   Professor Paul Schoemaker - Sloan Management Review

- *Identify Major Stakeholders*: Know who will have an interest in these issues, or influence them. Identify their current roles, interests and power positions and ask how have they changed over time, and why. For example, in environmental concerns, judges, journalists, scientists and regulators have become increasingly powerful.
- *Identify Basic Trends*: What political, economic, social, environmental, technological and legal trends are sure to affect the issues identified. Explain each trend and why it exerts influence on areas of concern. List each trend as positive, negative or uncertain influences.
- *Identify Key Uncertainties*: Consider political, economic, social, environmental, technological and legal factors, what events, with uncertain outcomes, will affect the issues being considered. (i.e. political election).
- *Construct Initial Scenario Themes*: Identify extreme worlds by putting all positive elements in one and all negatives in another. Alternatively, the various strings of possible outcomes can be clustered around high versus low continuity and degree of preparedness.
- *Check for Consistency*: These simple worlds created in the previous step are not yet fully fledged scenarios because they most likely contain internal inconsistencies. Need to remove these inconsistencies.
- *Develop Learning Scenarios*: General themes that are strategically relevant should start to emerge and the possible outcomes and trends should be organized around them.
- *Identify Research Needs*: It may be necessary, at this point, to conduct further research to flesh out the understanding of uncertainties and trends (i.e. new technologies not yet in the mainstream).
- *Develop Quantitative Models*: Re-examine internal inconsistencies of the scenarios and assess whether certain interactions should be formalized through

quantitative models. Such models can also help to quantify the consequences of various scenarios.

- *Evolve Towards Decision Scenarios*: Converge towards scenarios that will test strategies and generate new ideas.

In short, the main benefit of scenario planning is to explore the joint impact of various uncertainties which are given equal weighting. It is more realistic to the real world because it assumes that all variables, relating to a scenario, can change simultaneously and does not try to keep any of them constant for ease of evaluation.

2.4 Measures, Targets, and Initiatives

The results of another national survey conducted by W. Schiemann & Associates Inc. indicated that measurement plays an important role in translating business strategy into results. In fact, this survey found that organizations which are leaders in their industry with usually good financial performance distinguished themselves by the following *strengths* and exceptional characteristics:

- ✓ Clear and agreed-upon measures that managers understand.
- ✓ Good balance between financial and non-financial measurement.
- ✓ Strong link between strategic measures and operational measures.
- ✓ Frequent strategy update to reflect new variables.
- ✓ Good communication of measures to all employees.

For the above reasons, many companies are rediscovering the criticality of measurement as an important management tool. "You simply can't manage anything you can't measure," says Richard Quinn, vice president of quality at the Sears Merchandising Group. [41]

With regards to motivation, measures do help motivate an organization toward the strategic destination. Measures give individuals concrete links to the organization's strategy and its goals. In short, the following are the main *benefits* for using measures:

- ✓ Measures function as tools to drive desired behavior.
- ✓ Measures give individuals direction in what they need to accomplish for the organization's strategy.
- ✓ People respond to what's inspected, not what's expected.

---

41   John H. Lingle, From BSC to IS Measurement, 1/1/2007, Wm. Schiemann & Associates Inc.

According to Dennis Campbell, a good strategic plan includes solid set of measures that can translate strategy into understandable operational terms to employees. Usually, strategy fails to achieve this objective if they include too many or unaligned measures. Too many measures can weaken the focus on strategic objectives, making it difficult to communicate a consistent implementation plan to staff responsible for achieving those objectives. Moreover, a large list of measures that do not have clear linkages to the overall strategic objectives may be a sign of a larger problem: the lack of strategic focus at the top of the organization. Measures selected in any strategy should have clear and solid links to the overall performance objectives. Understanding the importance of different measures in driving these objectives is a necessary condition for providing good, actionable information at the operational level, where strategy is actually implemented.[42]

Perhaps it is fairly easy to find suitable financial measures for an organization, but this task is not that easy when applied to more subjective or vague areas (i.e. customer feedback, people development, and internal processes). To make measure selection more systematic, Pateman followed certain path in developing strategy measures. Pateman recommended first to have a flexible and creative mindset when developing measures. He argued that measures drive the behavioral changes required by the strategy. Measures cause staff to act differently; improve certain processes; and drive discussion and agenda items at executive-level. Well designed measures enable management to ask right questions, rather than give neat answers and results. In different words, measures are tools to create a climate for action and to support dynamic strategic discussion.[43]

---

42   Dennis Campbell,, Choose the right measures and drive the right strategy, 6/1/2006, Balanced Scorecard Report, pp. 14-16

43   Andrew J. Pateman,, Five easy steps for developing your BSC measures, 4/1/2004, Balanced Scorecard Report, pp. 15-17

Generally, there might be many possible measures for every objective. For each objective, Pateman suggested, that the project team should review the following while listing potential measures:

- Behavioral changes that this objective demands.
- Improvements requirements that needs to be done.
- Topics that executives need to discuss regarding the objective.
- Sources of measures already exist vs. needed to be established.

Filtering and selecting the best measures comes next. This step has two parts: First, the project team shortlists potential measures to ensure only the best ones remain. Pateman proposed using the following criteria to select measures that:

- Help managers understand strategic performance.
- Quantifiable and repeatable.
- Updated frequently enough to be meaningful (i.e. monthly).
- Help establish SMART targets (specific, measurable, aligned, realistic, and time-based).
- Encourage accountability.
- Strategic communication.
- Usefulness for target setting.

Second, top management could study this short list to select the most appropriate measures. Pateman suggested holding a half-day executive workshop for the selection process, in which executives collectively decide which measures to apply to each objective.[44]

---

44   Andrew J. P., Five easy steps for developing your BSC measures, 4/1/2004, Balanced Scorecard Report.

In the research conducted by W. Schiemann & Associates Inc. to understand how executives see "quality of measures" of the following six strategic performance areas, the outcomes are listed in Table 1.

Table 1: Quality of Measures for Strategic Performance Areas

Performance Area	Clearly Defined	Updated Semi-Annually
Financial performance	92%	88%
Operating efficiency	68%	69%
Customer satisfaction	48%	48%
Employee performance	17%	27%
Innovation/change	13%	23%
Community/environmental	25%	23%

S Source: W. Schiemann & Associates Inc

Research samples were based on the following two criteria:

- Measures are clearly defined.
- Measures are updated at least semiannually.

Most striking in these figures is how few managers feel that their organizations have been able to define in clear terms what the organization hopes to accomplish and measure in the areas of employee performance, innovation/change and community/environment. Even in the area of customer satisfaction, the data indicate there is disagreement in many companies on what should be measured. But on the other side, industry managers surveyed closely track financial performance and operating efficiency with stronger and clearer measures.[45]

Measures could have many unit forms. Each form has strengths and weaknesses, the most common forms are listed in Table 2.

---

45   John H. Lingle, From BSC to IS Measurement, 1/1/2007, Wm. Schiemann & Associates Inc, pp. 1-6

Table 2: Measures Unit List

Measure Form	Strength	Weakness
Absolute Numbers	Clear and simple; unambiguous	One dimensional, does not consider context
Indices	Allow multi-variate analysis	Masks underlying individual variables
Percentages	Good indicators of relative change, used over time	Sometimes misunderstood or improperly used
Rankings	Easy to compute and to understand objective	Category definitions often inconsistent
Ratings	Good for nominal data	Can be biased
Ratios	Depict critical relationships to be managed	Can be difficult to understand how to manage relationship

Source: Palladium Group

One way to categorize measures is by splitting them between "Lag" and "Lead":

- Lag measures: measures focus on the performance results at the end of a time period or activity.
- Lead measures: measures focus on how the organization wants the objective to be achieved by looking at intermediate processes, activities, or behaviors.

Lag measures are generally standard within a specific industry. Whenever possible and reasonable, the organization should use the industry generic measures that already exist and not spend valuable time inventing measures when existing measures are available.

Lead measures reflect the strategic position that the organization wants to take. It is sometime useful when top management wants to communicate and measure the way they want things done throughout the organization. Lead measures communicate the "how" of the strategy. Lead measures are especially useful to identify the kinds of behavior needed to achieve the objectives. They are necessary, but alone are not sufficient to achieve the organization's objectives. It is very common to see strategic plans contain a mix of both lag and lead measures.

The following are some typical *difficulties* in developing measures within an organization:

- ✘ It may be difficult to get cross-functional and credible representation.
- ✘ Insufficient availability of data.
- ✘ Measures may not clearly communicate the intent behind the objectives.
- ✘ There may be too many measures.
- ✘ There may be a lack of agreement on measures.

A well-designed strategic plan requires establishing of targets that are designed to stretch and push the organization forward in meeting its strategic objectives. One common place to start in setting a target is to look at past performance and current baselines. Past trends can be extended for modest improvement. Also, strategic goals can give organization clues as to what targets should be in its strategic plan. Another good source for targets is benchmarking for best practices. The main purposes of setting targets are to:

- Help an organization sets and communicates the expected level of performance. Most departments and individuals focus more clearly when given a quantifiable goal.
- Serve as a link between the department/individual and the organizational strategy/goal. Most individuals in an organization don't know the performance level

necessary to ensure the success of the organization's strategy.

- Help focus the organization on improvement. Simply defining a measure tells staff how management will measure performance, but it does not communicate the expected level of improvement required to achieve the strategy.

- Motivate the organization, not to control or constrain it. Although target setting is organizationally and culturally determined, it is recommended that targets are achievable.

Targets need to be realistic so that people feel comfortable about trying to execute. In most cases, targets should be mutually agreed upon between management and the person held responsible for hitting the target. When setting effective targets, managers must strike a balance between setting the bar high enough to encourage greater performance without prompting risky behavior; and leaving loopholes that allow people to game the system. According to John Langwith, managing director of analysis, planning, and reporting in TD Ameritrade, the company has to be comfortable in setting growth targets. He added that "if you want people to reach 200, set the target at 300, not 205". Furthermore, says Langwith, "If you create a difficult target, you force people to think outside the box - to make them think hard about their business model. Setting stretch targets make you continually challenge the way your base model is set."[46] Most used criteria for setting targets are described in the following list:

- Set only one target per measure for a certain time. More than one target will cause confusion within the organization and may communicate an unfocused strategy, theme, and objective.

---

46   Janice Koch, The challenge of target setting, 8/1/2007, Balanced Scorecard Report, pp. 14-16

- Ensure that targets are quantifiable. Targets that are not quantifiable can lead to subjective evaluation later on in the process. Based on the frequency of evaluation, it must be clear whether the target was met or not.
- Ensure that the target clearly communicates expected performance. There must be no doubt as to what performance is expected of the organization.
- Show the relationship between the target and the corresponding measure, objective, and strategy.

Common *weaknesses* in setting targets are listed next:

- ✗ Targets do not represent a balance between being realistic and challenging.
- ✗ It is not achievable within the approved resources.
- ✗ Data can not be collected and reported against targets.
- ✗ Is not expressed in a clear and simple way.
- ✗ Stakeholders do not regard the targets as appropriate.
- ✗ It is not aligned with strategic objectives.

It is worth noting that targets could have disadvantages in terms of setting direction to employees. Employees could focus on what is expected and not necessary what is needed to be done. Each organization needs to consider the expertise behind the target-setting and what potential behavior would result from people who are in charge of making things happen. It is also common today to use stretch targets for the following reasons:

- Set long-term performance goals for the organization. They are typically set within an appropriate strategy timeframe of three to five years.
- Keep an organization focused on the long-term strategy, while working on shorter-term goals.
- Identify areas in which an organization may require dramatic change and improvement. It communicates to the organization the need for change.
- Align with the organization's planning horizon.

There are many methods used by organization to help management in target setting process. Typical target setting methods include:

- *Derived from Business Goal*: Many times the overall business goals are prescribed by the market or by corporate shareholders. In this case, the organization does not really have a choice; it is a derived strategy.
- *Benchmark Industry Leaders*: Most organizations strive to be number one or two in their industry. Identify those companies that are number one or two and identify their methods for achieving success.
- *Improvement Based on Historical Performance*: Most organizations use this method to build their budgets. However, this method has serious flaws, as it does not take into account the changing competitive environment.
- *Establish Baseline and Define Targets Over Time*: This target setting approach is typically used with new measures and desired targets. When there is no basis for defining the performance level required (target), many organizations will allow operational monitoring to set a baseline of performance before setting the target.
- *Derived from Customer Expectations*: Where the customer expectations set the target for the organization.

It is important at this time to emphasis on the relationship between targets. When setting targets, it is essential to remember the relationships between targets. Setting one target inappropriately can cause varied effects on other targets. The goal should be to set targets in such a way that each individual measure is optimized to result in the best overall outcome for the organization. Setting targets can be *difficult* for many reasons:

✗ No historical data exists, or the measure is new to the organization.
✗ Autonomy for developing targets rest only with top leadership.
✗ Fear and anxiety of measures/targets is an emotional barrier.
✗ Future reward and compensation aspects can also pose a major challenge.

In regards to target ranges, according to Juan Andalaft, Director of Corporate Budgeting and Controlling at Endesa Corporation, who explained that well studied and carefully set ranges for targets are required for successful implementation of any strategic plan, for example:[47]

· 0% to 75% (equal to red/poor)
· 76% to 99% (equal to yellow/below target)
· 100% and over (equal to green/on or over target)

Langwith notes that each target has its normal historical variability. For instance, a target driven by external factors will have much wider variability. Irregularity becomes important factor in designing target ranges, in turn outstanding and poor performance are not central from the target. Langwith explained "that 200 target would have lower range of 195, which means only 5 points are needed to trigger a red flag, while it takes 25 to trigger good performance". For this reason "Overall range is determined by variability -and establishes the minimum below and above. How close to that minimum management set the threshold or outstanding mark is based on the degree of difficulty the target represents, as well as the severity of a miss

---

and the importance of overachieving." He added that if missing a target has serious consequences, the company will set a narrow range beneath the target. [48]

Initiatives help close the gap between current and desired performance. Initiatives enable the organization to align resources (i.e. people, time, money, equipment) to the strategic direction. Organizations often use the terms "initiative," "project," and "program" without clarifying the difference, which causes confusion. According to standard definitions that were set by "Project Management Institute's Guide" to the "Project Management Body of Knowledge":[49]

- *Project* is "A temporary endeavor undertaken to deliver a unique product, service, or result." A project has a definite scope, specific start and completion dates, and a distinct cost.
- *Program* is "A set of related projects managed in a coordinated way," which we qualified with "to achieve benefits or synergy that cannot be achieved by managing them individually."
- *Strategic Initiative* is "An integrated set of programs and/or projects managed in a coordinated way and aimed at building core or differentiating business capability."

Initiative is a project or a program outside of an organization's day-to-day operational activities that is meant to help the organization achieve its strategy. An initiative could address things like organizational change, capability improvement, performance enhancing, cost cutting, workforce training and process re-engineering/documentation.

48   Janice Koch, The challenge of target setting, 8/1/2007, Balanced Scorecard Report, pp. 14-16
49   Terry S. Brown and Matthew R. Gill,, Charting New Horizons with Initiative Management, 10/1/2008, Balanced Scorecard Report, pp. 13-16

According to Terry Brown and Matthew Gill, initiatives are the heart of any strategic plans. This is the most critical area of strategy management. He noted that many organizations have *difficulties* with their initiatives at different stages, such as:

- ✗ Defining what they are.
- ✗ Testing them for strategic alignment.
- ✗ Planning and prioritizing them.
- ✗ Tying them to the budget.
- ✗ Managing them effectively.

Many past publications made the connection that if one company executes initiatives successfully it will be able to execute its strategy successfully. Even it sounds like a simple equation, it is not that easy. According to a 2007 Global Survey done by Palladium Group:[50]

- • 79% of respondents believe their organizations are either "OK" or worse at ensuring that initiatives are well aligned to the strategy.
- • 69% rated their organizations "OK" or worse at holding executives responsible for their initiatives.

LaCasse argued that if the purpose of initiatives is to implement strategy, then the organization must first ensure any initiative under consideration is aligned with key organizational goals and objectives. He proposed three steps for initiatives development:

- ✓ Identify and collect potential initiatives.
- ✓ Evaluate and prioritize potential initiatives.
- ✓ Plan and approve initiative implementation.

Palladium Group suggested in their Performance Management 2007 December report that the best initiative ideas come from

---

50   Peter LaCasse, Initiative Management - Putting Strategy into Action, 12/1/2007, Performance Management, pp. 7-13

operations and staff. For this reason, it's important to create bottom-up channel that allow the initiative ideas to flow freely from employees. Such channel allows management to get good ideas. For instance, some advanced companies today use intranet to speed the flow of ideas from all sources to decision makers. These companies even established procedures for managers to solicit ideas and to encourage employees who propose good ideas with big rewards. Initiative identification and collection process is summarized in the following steps:

- An employee writes a description and objective of a potential initiative, an explanation of how it aligns to the strategy, and benefit-cost assessment.
- First-level management screen and filter potential initiatives.
- Management reviews submissions and selects potential initiatives they believe deserve sponsorship.
- Management appoints a sponsor from its ranks to lead potentially worthwhile initiative ideas.

After ideas are identified, collected, and assigned a sponsor, next is to evaluate each idea and prioritize the pool of ideas. This is done by using an established set of criteria to ensure objectivity. A fact-based approach makes it easier for management to decide what to support. Management is more comfortable supporting initiatives when politics are removed from the decision-making process and decisions are based entirely on objective information. This comfort level is critical, since initiatives commonly require coordination and collaboration across the organization. Initiative evaluation and prioritizing process is summarized in the following steps:

- Management uses standard criteria with which to rank and evaluate each initiative. This review often includes financial and strategic return, resource demands, and risks considerations.

- Management works to build a priority list, using facilitation techniques to build consensus (i.e. vote, mediate disagreement)
- Management identifies initiative managers so they can begin planning.

Initiative plans naturally vary in detail, depending on the scope and complexity of the initiative. Once an initiative has received priority ranking, its implementation must be planned. Planning helps organizations better manage their critical resources during any given time period. Initiative planning and approval process is summarized in the following steps:

- Initiative managers define the purpose of the initiative and demonstrate its alignment to strategic and operational objectives.
- Initiative managers define what resources will be needed, and how and from where they will be allocated; outline project management, stipulating personnel, milestones, and deliverables; assess the cost/benefit tradeoff; identify risks; and establish a start date.
- Initiative sponsor and leadership team members review and approve the initiative plan to ensure all questions are addressed.
- Resources are allocated for approved initiatives and the initiative enters the project management phase. [51]

Strong organizations could effectively and efficiently turn ideas into action, translating the "what" described in the strategy into the "how" of strategic initiatives. First, this could be done by initiative planning where an organization draws its way to new and better destination. Second, by using strong initiative management process, companies can overcome obstacles and challenges. The whole process makes its management check,

---

51   P. LaCasse, Initiative Management - Putting Strategy into Action, 12/1/2007, Performance Management.

analyze, adjust course, and sometime change destinations altogether. [52]

Typical *challenges* in inventorying, and prioritizing initiatives are summarized bellow:

*   ✗   Can be difficult to collect initiatives.
*   ✗   The existence of too many initiatives.
*   ✗   Don't understand the impact or dependencies between initiatives and the objectives they support.
*   ✗   Organizational politics and hidden agendas.
*   ✗   Natural anxiety surrounding cut backs.

Common *weaknesses* in strategic initiatives identification, planning, and execution process are listed next:

*   ✗   They are business as usual activities.
*   ✗   Accountability does not exist at the middle-management level.
*   ✗   Start and stop dates and progress milestones are not clearly defined.
*   ✗   Deliverables are not clearly defined.
*   ✗   Required resource allocation is not committed (i.e. real employee hours).
*   ✗   Too little attention to breaking implementation into manageable steps.
*   ✗   Evaluation of proposals driven by initial price rather than long-term value for money (especially securing delivery of business benefits).
*   ✗   Lack of understanding of industry at senior levels in the organization.
*   ✗   Lack of effective project team integration between clients, the supplier team, and the supply chain.

---

52   UK Office of Government Commerce Best Practice

✘ Lack of clear links between the project and the organization's key strategic priorities, including agreed measures of success.

✘ Lack of clear senior management and Ministerial ownership and leadership.

✘ Lack of effective engagement with stakeholders.

✘ Lack of skills and proven approach to project management and risk management.

2.5 Vertical and Horizontal Alignment

Soichiro Honda, founder of the Honda Motor Company, described that the most important obligations of senior leadership is to set a "Vision" to communicate what will the company be in the future, and to set four or five "Goals" that employees can contribute to and align to. Alignment is a necessary condition for organizational effectiveness. "Alignment" here is defined by Fonvielle and Carr "by having a common agreement about goals and means. On the largest scale, alignment is the achievement of goal congruency where all parts and functions of an organization's value chain work toward the same purpose". In its ideal form, all members of the organization can align their personal values and objectives with those of the firm. Fonvielle and Carr added that alignment is not only a matter of individuals agreeing on goals and means; it also refers to the need for business processes and functions to rally their actions around the organization's strategy. The strategic alignment process must start at the top level of the organization and "cascade" down, unifying direction for units and functions, teams, and ultimately individuals. [53]

According to John Lingle, 74% of measurement-managed companies reported that unit performance measures were linked to strategic company measures. In addition, 52% of the companies took it one step further and linked individual performance measures to unit performance measures. Effective organizations are integrated entities in which different units, functions and levels support the company strategy and one another.[54]

---

53   William Fonvielle and Lawrence P. Carr, Gaining Alignment - Making Scorecards Work, 1/3/1999, Management Accounting, pp. 1-12

54   John H. Lingle, From BSC to IS Measurement, 1/1/2007, Wm. Schiemann & Associates Inc, 1-6

For strategy to become meaningful to employees, their personal goals and objectives must be aligned with the organization's objectives. Communication provides individuals with a broad understanding of company and business-unit strategy. It makes explicit where employees fit in to the organization's strategy maps and how they can contribute to strategic objectives. A best practice in personal goal alignment is establishing individual objectives that are cross-functional and longer-term. There are many ways to link individuals' behavior to higher-level business-unit and corporate objectives. Successful organizations will share with employees the strategy and results they are trying to achieve, and will allow each individual or team to define personal objectives they can attain that will effect organizational results.[55]

To capture the full benefits of operating a multi-business, multi-function organization, executives must link company strategy to the strategies of their business and functional units. Top managers need to ensure that all business units are aligned. Strategy is usually defined at the business-unit level. But companies typically consist of multiple business or operating units. Corporate-level strategy defines how the strategies of individual business units can be integrated to create synergies not available to business units that operate independently from each other. Corporate strategy is described by a strategy map that identifies the specific sources of synergies. Managers then cascade this map vertically to business. [56]

In addition, managers need to align support units with business-unit and corporate strategies. Executives often treat support units and corporate staff functions as flexible expense centers, that is, as overhead departments whose goals are to

---

55   David P. Norton and Randall H. Russell,, Motivate to Make Strategy Everyone's Job, 12/1/2004, Balanced Scorecard Report, pp. 2-5

56   Dr. Robert Kaplan & David Norton, Integrated Strategy Planning and Operational Execution A Six-Stage System, 6/1/2008, Balanced Scorecard Report, pp. 2-6

minimize their operating expenses. As a result, the strategies and operations of support units do not align well with those of the company and the business units they are supposed to support. Successful strategy execution requires that support units align their strategies to the value-creating strategies of the company and its business units. Support units should negotiate service-level agreements with business units to define the set of services they will provide. Creating support unit strategy based on the service-level agreements enables each unit to define and execute a strategy that enhances the strategies being implemented by business units.[57]

There are several cascade methods used among corporate office, business units, and support units to vertically align corporate strategy:

- *Identical*: Corporate, business units, and support units share identical objectives. The greatest benefit of using the identical cascading method is clarity. Corporate knows exactly what and how the business unit will carry out their part of the corporate strategy. On the other hand, organizations with a decentralized style of management, or with relatively independent business units, may find this approach less appealing. To force-fit an objective and measure onto a unit where its relevance is suspect may bring into question the viability of the approach in the organization.
- *Contributory*: business units and support unit shares objectives translated from corporate. When using a contributory method, business unit contributes a piece of the entire process that corporate is trying to measure. The business unit objectives are localized, but matching with the corporate objectives. The strength of the contributory method is the independence and interpretation it allows individual

---

57   R. S. Kaplan, "The Demise of Cost and Profit Centers," BSR January–February 2007

units within the enterprise. It accommodates a more decentralized organizational approach, and works well when the "how" is best determined at a lower level in the organization. The trade-off to this approach is loss of control at the corporate level. It can also be harder to ensure that the sum of the various business and support unit strategies actually will produce the corporate strategy.

- *New*: Objectives that do not link directly to those on the corporate level. New objectives can exist on all types of strategy, but they are more typical in a holding company, where strategies are rarely built in as much detail as an operating company.

Vertical alignment results from cascading the strategy from the corporate level downward to business units, and upward to the board of directors. This vertical cascade downward allows the business units, which are the building blocks of customer value, to offer a unique combination of products or services that creates value for end customers. The vertical cascade upward allows the board of directors to make effective decisions. Business units, when properly aligned, provide everyone an understanding of his/her role in executing the organization's strategy, and provide everyone in the organization a clear visibility of the strategy. Most strategy cascade methods begin with corporate, then business units, and then support units. However, timing of the cascades changes, and time required to complete each cascade is generally reduced over time.

One tool is commonly used to align business units' objectives with corporate objectives is objectives matrix template. The business units and corporate organization use an objectives matrix template to visually clarify the relationship between business units and corporate organization objectives. With an understanding of the parent strategy, the business units will build a strategy map to align and support the corporate strategy. This strategy map will consist of linked objectives.

Aligning every individual in the enterprise and the development of personal objectives will take getting used to by the organization, and is a very big task to try to accomplish all at once. The organization should consider phasing in the deployment of personal objectives. The sequence would logically follow the priority for strategy.

- ✓ Start with aligning only the executive team to the strategy.
- ✓ Create personal objectives for strategic jobs, which have a high impact on strategy.
- ✓ Cascade the system to the rest of the employees.

A very small percentage of jobs have a significant impact on strategy and enterprise performance. The organization must focus resources first on jobs that differentiate the enterprise in the marketplace. Strategic Jobs are the positions in which employees with the right skills, talent, and knowledge have the biggest impact on enhancing the organization's critical internal processes.

First, for each of the strategic jobs, the organization should document and assess the skills, knowledge, and values required for success in that job. Definition of these items for all the identified strategic jobs creates the competency profile for those jobs. The next assessment step is to determine if and how well the individuals in those jobs possess the requirements detailed in the competency profile. Next, a development plan will need to be created to close a strategic skill gap.

Horizontal alignment results from cascading the strategy from corporate/business unit levels, to support units and external partners. Support units and external partners are generally considered to be organizations that support the strategic businessunits in daily operations and ultimately the achievement of strategy. A cascaded strategy ensures that support unit and external partner activity supports the strategy of the business units and the enterprise. If the organization works closely with external partners such as suppliers and distributors, it may be appropriate to define the strategic relationship with them.

The resources provided by support units such as human resources, information technology, purchasing and distribution are fundamental to strategic success. Studies show that support organizations are aligned with their organization's strategy only one third of the time. So while the organization and its business units may have a defined and aligned strategy, without support unit support, there are obvious obstacles to achieving strategy.[58]

It is important to note that many support units may have internal systems and processes that are clear, well-organized and logical in their structure. However, efficient, well-qualified support units do not necessarily contribute to the organization's strategy. Without this contribution, the organization will not achieve the synergies inherent in strategic alignment.

In general, it is easier to cascade to a business unit than to a support unit. Business units are typically revenue-generating profit centers. Usually, these units understand strategy and strategic objectives. The critical factor is the alignment of support units. Support units have to learn how they are strategic to the organization. Once they can define their strategic contributions, it is important that they ensure the parent organization agrees. Once the larger organization agrees, the support unit must communicate their value as effectively as possible. This communication will help pave the way for changes, alignments, and a new way of doing business.

---

58   CIO Insight/Balanced Scorecard Collaborative (BSCol), Society for Human Resource Management (SHRM)/BSCol study, 2002

Third party alignment is generally accomplished with a Service Level Agreement (SLA), although they are often utilized with support units within an organization as well. Horizontal alignment with an external partner is generally attempted in order to:

- Educate the third party about organizational objectives.
- Define how the third party contributes toward those objectives, and appropriate measures.

A service-level agreement (SLA) is a negotiated agreement between two parties where one is the customer and the other is the service provider. This can be a legally binding formal or informal 'contract'. The SLA records a common understanding about services, priorities, responsibilities, guarantees and warranties. Each area of service scope should have the 'level of service' defined. The SLA may specify the levels of availability, serviceability, performance, operation, or other attributes of the service such as billing. The 'level of service' can also be specified as 'target' and 'minimum', which allows customers to informed what to expect (the minimum), whilst providing a measurable (average) target value that shows the level of organization performance. It is important to note that the 'agreement' relates to the services the customer receives, and not how the service provider delivers that service.

Service level agreement could play the role of performance contract between business units and support units. Parties can then understand the strategic context of their performance objectives. In this way, support units can be rewarded for strategy contribution.

In defining this customer relationship, in support of horizontal alignment, many organizations find it helpful to create a service level agreement, which acts as a mechanism to support the contractual enforcement of the strategy execution.

The service level agreement is generally comprised of the key measures. It does clarify and provides a "contract" between the operating unit, the internal customer, and support unit. Service level agreements define the value that the internal customer desires from the support unit and how they measure the delivery of that value. Service level agreements are not unusual, but are not mandatory either.

External partners are generally outside third-party organizations that support the enterprise in daily operation and ultimate achievement of strategy. They can also be external organizations that have an interest or stake in the performance of the enterprise. Typical external partners may include investors, customers, distributors, joint ventures, vendors, suppliers, new ventures, outsourcers, and government agencies.

The most important and critical items on the strategy alignment check list are designed to address the content, process, and impact of alignment of the strategic plan during cascading phase. The recommended *check list* items are as follows:

- ✓ For organization that contains distinct business units, the strategy provides a good template for the development of business unit strategies.
- ✓ Corporate objectives been used to develop business unit/divisional objectives.
- ✓ The cascade process has been effective.
- ✓ Business units and divisions can see how they contribute to corporate strategy.
- ✓ Support units understand how they contribute to business unit and divisional strategies.
- ✓ Strong alignment in contributing to corporate goals.
- ✓ Improved synergy between the corporate strategy and business unit strategy with clear link.
- ✓ Alignment across business units enabled easier identification of corporate goals.

✓ Better identification of cross-impact areas between business units.

✓ Alignment process enabled improved clarity of services delivered.

✓ Alignment process enabled better cross-selling of services across business units.

✓ Alignment process improved relationships between divisions and support units within the organization.

✓ Strong link between manpower plans to strategy.

✓ Link competency development plan to strategy in order to bridge the gap between current situation and future situation.

✓ Link organization structure to strategy.

✓ Link finance factors to strategy.

✓ Individual performance plans linked to strategy.

✓ Clear breakdown of strategic projects into specific activities with assigned responsibilities on both department and individual level.

✓ Approved authorities and responsibilities matrix to help all units in achieving the overall strategic objectives.

With regards to public sector, there are many challenges in coordinating government departments' actions and services in a synergized and unified way. This lack of horizontal alignment across the government agencies is causing overlap and waste of resources. The following common *weaknesses* with horizontal alignment in the public sector are listed below:

✗ The communication between departments is not strong.

✗ Difficulty in identifying the right channels to communicate.

✗ Communication channels within and between departments is weak and needs to be improved through the establishment of specialized communication units.

✘ No common set of tools identified and implemented to facilitate and enhance the planning alignment process.
✘ No reliable and accurate data to assist with the strategy development, and online tools that will assist with the strategic planning process.
✘ Cumbersome administrative planning process.

Improvement *ideas* to help improve cross-departmental issues are included in the following list:

✓ Ensure that middle management plays an important role in inter-departmental communication.
✓ Detailed identification of communications channels, points of contact and core services to be provided based on MOUs.
✓ Establish an inter-departmental communications framework and plan that ensures two-way communication is transparent.
✓ Hold regular workshops or government forums to share experiences and information.
✓ Government call centre to address departments queries.
✓ The creation of a government department responsible for clarifying mandates, and providing information and data.
✓ Hold a workshop prior to the start of the strategic planning process to communicate the required time-frames, deliverables, introduce the planning cycle and train the responsible departments using a local case-study approach.
✓ Identify and agree on government-wide strategic policy.
✓ Need to articulate and agree on sector based outcomes.
✓ Have some form of performance agreement with the head of departments and agencies.

- ✓ Explain the department or agency's 'statement of intent' and intended actions of the entity and its perceived capability.
- ✓ Integrated fiscal management and application of output-based budgeting.
- ✓ Clear and concise documents covering intent and subsequent measurement of performance against agreed expectations.
- ✓ Separate sector-based sessions addressing issues related to specific sector.
- ✓ Emphasized sector based policy responsibility and integration.
- ✓ Effective and clear accountability, responsibility, and delegation of authority.
- ✓ Continuing and effective communication.
- ✓ Establish data center for easy access to relevant, timely, and research data.

2.6 Linking Strategy to Budget and Resources

Most organizations recognize that there is a significant gap between their strategic plans and their ability to execute. Part of the reason for this was shown in a survey conducted by CFO Research Services where 60 percent of organizations said they were dissatisfied in the alignment between strategy and budget.[59] This alignment is vital because the budget is often the only enterprise-wide process where users are directed and controlled in their use of company assets to achieve organizational objectives.

Resourcing a strategic plan involves providing the people, money, and materials to ensure successful implementation. Many organizations link the strategic plan with the budgeting process at the initial strategic planning session or soon afterward when they create implementation plans. Some choose to have implementation managers identify resources and present them to top management for approval. This helps top management to prioritize implementation actions and allot resources to move the organization toward achieving its strategic goals.

Gary Hamel and C.K. Prahalad published a book called "Competing for the Future". The authors summed up this disconnect in their book in a powerful statement that said: "In too many companies there is a grand, and overly vague, long-term goal on one hand; and detailed short-term budgets and annual plans on the other hand; with nothing in between to link the two together. The long term doesn't start at year five of the current strategic plan. It starts right now!"[60]

---

59   CFO Research Services and Comshare, Incorporated, What CFOs Want from Per-
      formance Management, March 2003, pp. 6
60   Gary Hamel and C.K. Prahalad, Competing for the Future, Harvard Business
      School Press, 1994, pp. 120-121

Today, most organizations rely on the budget process to bridge the gap. Managers are told the needed results that are required for next year and in turn they develop a revenue/cost budget to achieve them. But this process is usually not linked with strategy, providing little direction as to how strategies are to be achieved, little analysis as to whether budgeting activities make sense given the current overall strategic plan, and little thought for conflicts between activities and resource allocation. Instead, the "how" of strategy management is either assumed or worked out as the year progresses and failures exist.[61]

A budget is typically defined as an organization's projected revenue and expenditures for the coming year. Budget includes capital investments (i.e. equipment), human capital (i.e. labor-direct), information capital (i.e. IT), process improvements (i.e. Six Sigma, TQM), inventory, and overhead (i.e. labor-indirect, administration). The budget is the point at which strategy connects to the reality of managing limited resources. Making informed decisions around the budget is critical and the strategy can support this process. Budgets are typically developed at the enterprise level, as well as at the business unit and support unit levels. It is important to build a strategic plan that could be implemented by available resources and capabilities.

According to Jack Welch, former GE chief, who once characterized budget as "the bane of corporate America," these words reflect the frustration of growing numbers of managers with budgeting process. For most companies, the annual budget process is a painful, distracting, and long exercise that consumes a lot of time and resources. Usually, the result of the budget process becomes outdated so quickly that it is often becomes irrelevant for decision making. In addition, since most organizations do not link the operational activities to strategy, they face fiscal disconnect. Once the budget is approved, they

---

61   Performance Management, Strategy Management and the Balanced Scorecard, 4/1/2007, GEAC

spend the next twelve months reconciling results to the original numbers. Despite the cost and complexity, the end result does not help the organization to adapt to changing conditions. Dr. David Norton identified financial budget as a controlled way to allocate financial resources that can be tracked and utilized with reasonable effectiveness. Financial budget is not a strong tool to promote a long-term view. It was not meant for communicating strategy or for target setting. In short, financial budget is a necessary tool for managing the allocation of financial resources. To manage strategy and operations, the organization must use other systems.[62]

Jack Welch, CEO of GE, said once in Fortune Magazine article (29 May 1995) that "The budget never should have existed. A budget is this: if you make it, you generally get pat on the back and a few bucks. If you miss it, you get a stick in the eye - or worse…."). Traditional budgeting is ineffective and rapidly becoming obsolete due to its inability to motivate the right behaviors, and its lack of harmony with strategic planning, because of the following reasons:

- ✘ It is static and based on an annual cycle.
- ✘ It takes too long to develop.
- ✘ It creates too much detail, waste, and inefficiency.
- ✘ It does not account for changing market conditions.

Many top managers wants their companies to be more adaptable to change, they may not know how to turn that desire into operating reality. They might seek fast response, innovation, process improvement, customer focus, and shareholder value. But their management processes, including plans, targets, measures, and rewards, all too easily remain stuck in old-fashioned ways of command and control that keep them

62   David P. Norton, Philip W. Peck,, Linking Operations to Strategy and Budgeting, 10/1/2008, Balanced Scorecard Report, pp. 1-6

from responding to today's needs. According to recent SAP study, traditional budget can be a *weakness* to:[63]

* ✗ *Fast Response*: Responding quickly to changing environments is difficult if the organization restricts itself to fixed annual strategies and budgeting cycles. Management relies on rules, procedures, and budgetary controls that constrain its freedom to act locally.

* ✗ *Finding and Keeping Talented People*: Hierarchical structures that are governed by rigid plans and inflexible financial budgets offer motivated managers limited opportunities for challenge, risk and reward, and personal development. Because they are designed to control, rigid plans and budgets do not encourage entrepreneurial leadership and risk taking.

* ✗ *Innovation*: Bloated bureaucracies and rigid budgetary controls often obstruct insight and innovation. They suppress creativity by failing to provide the management climate in which creative people thrive. When fixed budgets are the only target against which their performance is measured, managers are unprepared to aim high. Easy-to-achieve targets and overly cautious strategies are the result, and sooner or later, the company will begin to underachieve.

* ✗ *Operational Excellence*: One of the best opportunities for cost reduction is to adopt a flat management structure, within which the business processes interact at high speed, enabling managers to respond quickly to customer requests. But in the traditional budgeting model, resources and costs are hard-wired into the fabric of the business structure. Only by eradicating the old-fashioned budgeting mentality can organization encourage managers to challenge fixed costs and seek continuous cost reductions.

---

63   Beyond Budgeting - SAP, 1/1/2001, SAP Software

* *Close Relationships with Customers*: When salespeople are focused solely on achieving fixed targets for revenue, product volume, or gross margin, they have little incentive to care about whether the organization is meeting customers' needs or whether customers are satisfied and profitable.
* *Achieving Sustainable, Competitive Corporate Results*: One of the aims of the budgeting process is to produce earnings forecasts and set shareholders' expectations. Blind allegiance to financial targets and the budgets underlying them can cause long-term problems. Managers who set aggressive targets may be required to take drastic actions to meet shareholder's high expectations, such as downsizing, restructuring, and cutting of essential long-term investments in R&D.

After reading on this common issue between strategy and budget alignment, a conclusion could become visible that the most challenging part is to determine what should be included under strategic initiative vs. normal day to day operation. Dr. David Norton offered solution to link strategic funding requirements to the budget by creating a new category called "*Stratex*" to subsidize portfolios of strategic initiatives defined by the strategy management process. This simple addition to the traditional chart of accounts represents a revolutionary change in the way organizations manage its strategy budget.[64]

Dr. Norton also argues that it's not enough to allocate funding for strategy. Ideally, the budget should govern the allocation of resources to support both strategy and operations. To allocate all resources successfully, the organizations need a linkage mechanism that connects strategy and operations. In turn, he introduced new approach that provides this needed integration. It is called "Driver-Based Causal Model" that is constructed from

---

64   David P. Norton, Philip W. Peck, Linking Operations to Strategy and Budgeting, 10/1/2008, Balanced Scorecard Report.

key operational activity drivers that allow linking all resources (strategic, operational, and capital spending) to the operating plan. Driver-based causal model can:

- ✓ Simplify and transform the traditional budgeting process into an effective instrument of planning and strategy.
- ✓ Eliminate unnecessary detail and reduce the time and effort needed to create budgets.
- ✓ Provide transparency to the numbers and their underlying assumptions.
- ✓ Enable organizations to become more flexible and responsive to internal and external events.
- ✓ Help organization executes as well as perfects its strategy.
- ✓ Overcome many of the limitations of traditional budgeting.
- ✓ Use operational drivers to predict financial results.
- ✓ Represent the mathematical relationships between key operational drivers (i.e. call volume) and financial outcomes.
- ✓ Determine the cause-and-effect relationships among drivers, business activities, resource requirements, and financial outcomes.
- ✓ Improve planning and forecasting capabilities.

Budget emphasis today is on reporting actual results with budget variance analysis, in turn traditional budgeting looks at historical data. (i.e. plan vs. actual). It addresses only what happened. Based on 2005 study done by "IBM Institute for Business Value" shows that the ineffectiveness of the traditional budgeting is widely felt, only 42% of CFOs surveyed believe that their finance department measures and monitors business performance effectively. In fact, traditional planning focuses on minimizing deviation from the original budget and not on seeking proactive measures that can boost competitiveness and strategy success.[65]

According to research done by the American Quality and Productivity Center, 60% of organizations do not update their budgets regularly. In addition, fewer than 50% of organizations use a forecast horizon beyond the current quarter or fiscal year. Even though attention to short-term performance is important, obviously this doesn't support longer-term strategic objectives. Based on this limitation, Dr. David Norton suggested "Rolling Forecast". The rolling forecast, which began to appear in the mid-1990s, provides:

- ✓ Continuous performance outlook beyond the current year, generally five to six quarters from the present quarter.
- ✓ Directional indication of performance.
- ✓ Better estimate of expected future performance for both the short- and mid-terms.
- ✓ More focus on the key operational drivers with the greatest impact on financial performance.
- ✓ More flexibility and timeliness necessary for dynamic planning.
- ✓ Dynamic support, continuous planning and target setting.
- ✓ Quicker decision that can take action right away to mitigate expected shortfalls, or if performance surpasses expectations, resources can be freed up or reallocated to pursue other projects or opportunities.
- ✓ Support both operational and strategic management activities.
- ✓ Degree of visibility and flexibility not available in the typical planning process.

---

65   David P. Norton, Philip W. Peck,, Linking Operations to Strategy and Budgeting, 10/1/2008, Balanced Scorecard Report, pp. 5

The most difficult thing for organizations to do is to rationalize and reduce the amount of detail in budgets. Most companies believe that more detail equals more accuracy and this statement is completely false. More detail simply equals more resource effort, lengthy cycle times, and increased variance analysis.

The ability to adapt depends on business planning using a rolling forecast or a similar business planning process. This vehicle for continual planning, that includes adjusting execution priorities on an ongoing basis, is not a new concept. But it has been hampered by criticisms that it would prove too time consuming and difficult.

In general, rolling quarter forecasts allow an organization to continually adjust to changing conditions by revisiting targets, generally on a quarterly basis, as opposed to a yearly cycle. Continual adjustment of targets and resource allocations enables a more quick and responsive organization. Adapting oftentimes becomes important when reviewing strategy gaps and initiatives designed to bridge them. Initiatives are flexible activities implemented to help achieve targets.

Any gap between the forecast and the plan may require revisiting initiative priorities, or changing operational priorities and actions. For example, if a company forecasts a sales gap, it may launch new marketing programs (initiatives), accelerate or slow new product launches (operational priority), or redirect sales efforts in responsive markets (operational priority). Companies could budget/forecast on a summary line item basis (travel and expense) versus the detailed line item (rental car, lodging, etc.). By reducing the overall planning effort, it also becomes easier to integrate back upstream to the strategic planning process.

Most companies like to budget or forecast in the same level of detail across all possible dimensions of their organization. This can lead to an enormous amount of detail in the forecast and may paralyze an organization. An organization could assess the dimension in the forecast and rationalize the level of detail spent on each element. This is especially true if the organization is implementing a rolling forecast which commands to rationalize detail and match predictability with the forecast dimensions.

Another emerging model for budgeting is called Beyond Budgeting Model, It is designed to overcome traditional barriers and to create a flexible, adaptable organization that gives local managers self-confidence and freedom to think differently, make decisions rapidly, and collaborate on innovative projects with colleagues in multifunctional teams both within the company and outside it. Twelve principles provide a robust framework for implementing the Beyond Budgeting Model. As described below, principles 1 through 6 are concerned with the performance management climate at the company. They involve both the design of the organization and the delegation of power and responsibility to people who are close to the customers. Principles 7 through 12 are concerned with the processes of performance management. A key element is that goals, measures, and rewards are decoupled, that is, not tied together in a performance contract.[66]

- *Self-Governance*: Replace rules and procedures with clear values and boundaries to provide front-line managers with the freedom they need to make fast, effective decisions.
- *Performance Responsibility*: Recruit and develop the right people, those who have the mind-set to serve customers and take responsibility for achieving results.
- *Empowerment*: Delegate authority and responsibility to managers at the front line. Give decision-making power to managers who are close to the customers.

---

66   Beyond Budgeting - SAP, 1/1/2001, SAP Software

- *Structure*: Base new organization on a network of interdependent units with fast communication up, down, and across the business. Create as many small, entrepreneurial units as possible.
- *Coordination*: Design processes that work together naturally to deliver customer value. Use process and project based relationships to respond to customer demands in real time. When the company makes each unit responsible for its own results, market like forces driven by network of supplier customer agreements replace centralized control.
- *Leadership*: Challenge and stretch managers to make significant increases in performance and to break free from thinking only of small increments. Changed leadership style to coach and support managers, rather than command and control them.
- *Goal Setting*: Adopt relative, rather than absolute, targets and disconnected targets from measures and rewards. This will free local managers to set their sights on ambitious goals. Base relative targets on a range of key performance indicators and external benchmarks to encourage managers to pursue strategic as well as financial goals.
- *Strategy Process*: Free managers to think differently and to produce new ways of delivering customer value and to create new businesses altogether. Build new initiatives from strategic goals rather than from departmental concerns.
- *Anticipatory Systems*: Give managers early warning of changes that impact their businesses, particularly if the changes spell trouble ahead. Use rolling forecasts to keep an eye on the future. Anticipatory systems can help manage short-term capacity. If the organization integrates customer-order information with the supply chain, management needs not fix capacity far in advance, which turns some of fixed costs into variable ones.

- *Resource Utilization*: Delegate investment and resource decisions to people who are close to the action. Disconnect such decisions from the annual budgeting cycle to ensure that they are made only when needed and to give managers the freedom to take appropriate action at the right times. Maintain continuous downward pressure on costs by making efficient resource consumption highly visible within the company.
- *Measurement and Control*: Put into place comprehensive controls that provide actual results, leading indicators, and rolling forecasts, and support them with fast, open information systems. Disseminate measures to all management levels simultaneously, with more detail at a local level and less detail at a higher level.
- *Motivation and Rewards*: Base performance evaluations on relative measures to drive performance improvement. Emphasize performance by teams, groups, or companies, rather than individuals. This approach encourages sharing and ensures that the whole enterprise pulls in the same direction.

With regards to linking strategy to operation and processes, many of the organizations that adopt strategy management need to integrate their internal system with one or more of management disciplines. Today, the quality and process improvement encompasses many programs and methods. These tools are important in making process improvements, but they must be applied properly if they are to impact strategic objectives.

Process improvement methods, in the context of a strategy management system, are the most used via initiatives to help close performance gaps to strategy. Process improvement methods are used at a project level to improve performance and close gaps to achievement of strategy. The operational improvement methods noted below are generally oriented toward improving the efficiency (i.e. cost) and quality (i.e. conformance) of the processes to which they are applied. While implementation of these methods often requires an extensive organizational effort coupled with a lengthy implementation schedule, the results tend to be gained rapidly once the process improvement is started. The followings are common quality and process improvement methods:

- *Six Sigma*: Systematic, data-driven methodology using tools, training, measurements to enable product/ process design that meets customer expectations and can be produced at Six Sigma quality levels; emphasis on reduction of process variation.
- *Process Re-engineering*: Method of analysis & redesign of workflows within and between enterprises to streamline work processes and achieve improvement in quality, time management, and costs.
- *Lean Manufacturing*: Process management and tool set focused on the identification and reductions of 'wastes' in order to improve overall customer value, as well as to reduce production time and costs.

For organizations focused on executing a customer intimacy strategy, these process improvement methods are examples of ways to improve the processes that deliver this value. Whereas operation improvement approaches focus on efficiency and quality, customer intimacy improvement methods provide the tools needed to capture, interpret and distribute customer information in order to enhance the customer experience. These methods are effective but typically take longer to experience the results desired.

- *Total Quality Management (TQM)*: Management strategy aimed at embedding quality awareness in all organizational processes to create continual increase in customer satisfaction at continually lower real costs.

- *Customer Value Management*: Method of delivery optimal value to customers by aligning business metrics, capabilities, processes, organizational structure, infrastructure with customer-defined value.
- *Customer Life Cycle Management*: Measurement of customer relationship business performance over time; customer satisfaction, increase growth, enhance loyalty, decrease defections, optimize lifetime value, all the while reducing costs to serve.

Innovation processes are often the most difficult to improve. It's easy to test a product's quality and straight forward to gauge a customer's experience; determining how well an organization is innovating is harder especially since the results are typically not known until the product or service is introduced to the market, sometimes months or even years after conception. The methods identified below provide insights into ways an organization can improve its innovation processes, but innovation is often a long term commitment that extends, time-wise, beyond the period of time it takes to experience either operational excellence or customer intimate improvements.

- *Experience Co-Creation*: Management approach that highlights the value created at the point of interaction between companies and customers; enabled by technology interface devices.
- *Open Innovation*: Use of clear inflows and outflows of knowledge, establish 'creation nets' to accelerate innovation and to expand the markets for external use of innovation.

CHAPTER 3

STRATEGY MANAGEMENT & MONITORING METHODS

CHAPTER 3: STRATEGY MANAGEMENT & MONITORING METHODS

In today's economy, having a good business strategy is not enough to meet organizational goals. Organizations are struggling to implement strategy, streamline operations, and deliver more value to their customers. According to a Fortune magazine study, less than 10% of effectively developed organizational strategies were successfully implemented. In another study, Fortune found that when CEOs do fail, in more than 70% of cases it was not their strategy, but the execution of their strategy that was unsuccessful.[67]

Organizations are looking for new ways to optimize how they manage their business in order to improve execution on defined strategies. Quantitatively tracking and analyzing business activities has surfaced as an effective method in driving the proactive and predictive management of the business.

Monitoring business activities is not a new concept. In the 1970s, MIT coined the term Executive Information Systems. These were fourth-generation language; IT-centric decision support systems that provided a few executive managers with an organization's summarized financial data. While in trend for a time, these fell out of favor due to build and maintenance costs, inflexibility, and inability to deploy them beyond a few high-level executives.

According to Gartner, each methodology has its own strengths and weaknesses and no single methodology covers all organizational operations and departmental processes. Because of this, organizations often create larger Enterprise Performance Management (EPM) initiatives. EPM is also referred to as Business

---

67 Miyake, Dylan. "Implementing Strategy with the Balanced Scorecard: An Introduction to the Strategy-Focused Organization." DM Review, October 2002

Performance Management (BPM) or Corporate Performance Management (CPM). With EPM organizations often blend and create their own methodologies to improve cross department, enterprise-wide execution on defined strategies.[68]

Today, with resurging interest in information-driven management methodologies, organizations are taking interest in various methodologies for monitoring and driving business objective obtainment. The Balanced Scorecard (BSC) and EFQM Business Excellence Model remain popular strategic enterprise performance management methodologies, while other more tactic-specific methodologies include Outcome Based Management (OBM), the shareholder value centric like Value Based Management and Economic Value Added (EVA), and the Activity-Based Costing (ABC) accounting methodology.[69]

In summary, when an organization is practicing good and effective strategy management, thinking becomes more visionary, which is characterized by the following characteristics:

- ✓ Clear thinking about the future and organizational boundaries are more elastic.
- ✓ Change in focus from the inputs that are used to run the business to the outputs and outcomes the organization desires to achieve.
- ✓ More focus on optimizing organizational performance and process quality as keys to delivering quality products and services.
- ✓ Move toward an organizational culture that adapts easily to change.

---

68   Buytendijk, Frank and Rayner, Nigel. "A Starter's Guide to CPM Methodologies." Gartner, May 2002.

69   Rayner, Nigel. "CPM: A Strategic Deployment of BI Applications." Gartner, May 2002

Good practice and dedication of organizational learning through the application of strategy management will bring the organization closer to realizing its goals and vision. With each update of the strategic plan, top management will become better able to deploy the plan, implement changes, and measure organizational performance.

3.1 Balanced Scorecard

In the past, many methodologies were developed that sought to link internal and external activities of an organization, as well as cost and non-cost categories, to overall performance. The breakthrough methodology came with Norton and Kaplan's Balanced Scorecard. The Balanced Scorecard (BSC), developed in 1992 by Drs. David Norton and Robert Kaplan, has gained global acceptance as a powerful framework to help leaders define and implement strategy more effectively and efficiently. This is accomplished by translating the vision and strategy into a set of operational objectives that drive behavior and performance of the organization and its workforce. Balanced Scorecard gives top managers information from four different perspectives to help them focus more on important issues. The followings are related research data summaries that put Balanced Scorecard methodology ahead of other methodologies:

- Research suggests that 60 percent of Fortune 1000 companies have experimented with the Balanced Scorecard (Silk, 1998).
- Gartner Group suggests that over 50 percent of large US firms had adopted the Balanced Scorecard by the end of 2000.
- Data collected by the Balanced Scorecard potentially focus article collaborative suggest that of the firms not currently using the balanced scorecard, 43 percent are planning to use one soon and a further 48 percent are considering using one (Downing, 2001).
- The Balanced Scorecard Collaborative reported that based on a survey of the Hackett Group, for most users, 75% of their measures were financial and need to be more balanced.[70]

---

70   Philip Kirby & Sumner J. Schmiesing, Balanced Scorecards as Strategic Naviga-tional Charts - How to Implement Rapid Sustainable Change, 4/1/2003, Organiza-tion Thoughtware International & Visum Solutions, Inc., pp. 1-11

The Balanced Scorecard concept is built upon the premise that measurement motivates and that measurement must start with a clearly described and detailed strategy.[71] In summary, Balanced Scorecard is characterized by the following characteristics:

- Uses four perspectives which are used to describe the strategy (financial, customer, internal, and learning and growth).
- Has many performance measures that are clearly linked to the key strategies and priorities of the organization.
- Provides managers with a full and timely view of an organization's performance.
- Encourage managers to balance their actions between a short- and long-term focus.

The Balanced Scorecard approach starts from the organization's goals and priorities to address what it is trying to achieve in the long-term. From there it moves to ensure that the key strategic actions required to achieve these goals have been identified and planned for. Finally, it ensures that managers develop a comprehensive view of performance in the context of these plans by establishing measures across four inter-related perspectives: that of the customer, internal processes, learning and growth and financial performance.[72]

- *Financial Perspective*: Any organization requires key measures of its financial performance that need to be directly linked to the overall goals of the organization.
- *Customer Perspective*: An organization exists to provide services which meet the needs of its customers. It is critical that the organization has clear strategies for meeting customer needs and, in turn, has

71   Michael Nagel & Chris Rigatuso, Improving Corporate Governance: A Balanced Scorecard Approach, 1/1/2003, Balanced Scorecard Collaborative, pp. 4-11

72   Mike Wisniewski, The Measures of Success - Developing a BSC to measure performance, 6/1/1998, Accounts Commission for Scotland, pp. 5-7

performance measures that will help assess customer, and stakeholder, expectations, perceptions and levels of satisfaction.

- *Internal Process Perspective*. To provide quality and cost-effective services the organization must identify the key business processes it needs to be good at and then measure its performance in undertaking those processes.
- *Learning and Growth Perspective*: To achieve continuous improvement in delivering services to customers, organization needs to ensure that it is able to learn and to improve from both an individual and organizational standpoint.

Balanced Scorecard is more than simply a collection of performance measures grouped under these four perspectives and more than the usual financial performance measures supplemented by a few others. The scorecard needs to be developed and derived directly from the organization's declared vision and priorities. Traditionally, performance measures have focused mainly on financial information that reflects the results of current performance. For this reason, managers are pushed to make decisions that promote short-term value creation. Concern over this short-term focus has been an important issue because it may cause the manager to underemphasize activities that create value for the future. [73]

Robert Kaplan and David Norton developed the balanced scorecard as a performance measurement system to help mitigate this short-term decision-making focus. The balanced scorecard consists of measures linked to organization strategy and is structured to include a combination of financial measures that reflect past decisions and non-financial measures, which

---

73   Laurie Burney McWhorter, Does the Balanced Scorecard Reduce Information Overload, Summer 2003 Vol 4 No 4, Management Accounting Quarterly, pp. 23-27

are indicators of future performance. Therefore, the balanced scorecard should help managers to balance their decisions between short- and long-term gains.

An organization's strategy can be cause-and-effect relationships among organizational objectives. Because balanced scorecard includes both financial and non-financial measures, it provides a clear way to manage and verify the relationships expected between the measures and performance drivers. This direct link enables managers to perform their work more effectively, thereby helping them pursue organizational objectives. [74]

Balanced scorecard typically consists between four and seven measures for each of the four performance perspectives. This often results in up to 28 performance measures. If this volume is compared to a traditional performance measurement system where only a few financial outcomes are used, a concern arises about a manager's ability to process outcome information across so many dimensions. Kaplan and Norton contend that the number of measures in the balanced scorecard will not result in a system that is so complicated that managers' decision making is impeded because the balanced scorecard directs actions toward the pursuit of a unified strategy. The balanced scorecard's inclusion of multiple perspectives enables managers to group measures, which facilitates information processing and improve decision making. Because the ability to process information is an important element of information overload, this suggests that the balanced scorecard may help reduce the amount of information overload that a manager encounters. [75]

Balanced Scorecard architecture must reflect the environment in which the organization operates in. In the public sector,

---

74   Robert S. Kaplan and Anthony A. Atkinson. Advanced Management Accounting, 3rd edition, Prentice Hall, Upper Saddle River, N.J., 1998.

75   Marlyse Lipe and Steven Salterio, "A Note On The Judgemental Effects Of The Balanced Scorecard S Information Organization," Accounting, Organizations and Society, 2002, pp. 531-540.

the architecture reflects the achievement of outcome goal, and places a primary focus on satisfying the stakeholder, such as citizens. The Financial perspective is downgraded and sometimes renamed to Resources or Budget perspective to more adequately reflect the strategy, which is not financially driven. [76]

The use of cause and effect logic is the main differentiator between the Balanced Scorecard and other approaches to organizational measurement. Without the logical cause and effect linkages, the organization simply has "buckets of measures." Balanced Scorecard focuses the organization on the longer-term strategy, generally for the next three to five years. This shift moves the organization from a short-term management control system to a strategic management system.

In regards to alignment, by creating Balanced Scorecards at lower levels of the organization such as Strategic Business Units (SBU) and Shared Service Units (SSU) and by tying the Balanced Scorecard to the performance system for teams and individuals, an organization can assure good alignment of its strategy. This healthy alignment ensures that the actions of all employees are linked to the strategy. Main objectives of the Balanced Scorecard include:

- Translating strategy into operational terms.
- Ensuring that components of the strategy, objectives, measures, targets, initiatives, are linked and aligned.
- Communicating strategy throughout the organization.
- Forming the basis of an effective and integrated strategic management process.

In addition, Balanced Scorecard enables an effective strategic management process to link operational learning with strategic

---

76   Robert S. Kaplan, "Overcoming the Barriers to Balanced Scorecard Use in the Public Sector," Balanced Scorecard Report, Nov/Dec 2002

learning. The strategic learning loop gives the organization the ability to continually test strategy hypotheses. This flexibility allows the organization to keep up with the external environment. The ability to change quickly is particularly helpful for organizations that are in fast-paced industries. There are six steps in the Balanced Scorecard development process, they are:

- Define strategic destination.
- Identify key themes driving the strategy.
- Build strategic objectives & linkages.
- Determine measures and targets.
- Inventory, map and select priority initiatives.
- Report performance.

In summary, the main *benefits* that Balanced Scorecard practitioners generally expect for their organization include:

- ✓ Clarifying the vision.
- ✓ Gaining consensus and ownership.
- ✓ Aligning the organization.
- ✓ Integrating strategic planning.
- ✓ Driving resource allocation.
- ✓ Improving management effectiveness.
- ✓ Integrating multiple management tools and change initiatives.

Nonetheless the Balanced Scorecard is proving increasingly popular with organizations. By 1999 a Bain and Co. study reported that 50% of North American and 40% of European companies were using a Balanced Scorecard.

Critics however, point out that the Balanced Scorecard by starting with the strategy neglects the importance of key stakeholders such as suppliers, crucial to business success in the modern networked environment. They argue for firstly engaging in debate with key stakeholders about the appropriateness of the strategy before beginning the process of definition and objective setting.

In addition, there is a lack of substantive evidence about the performance improvements from Balanced Scorecard use. This may be partly explained by the high rate of implementation failure. A number of studies on Balanced Scorecard implementation tend to agree on a failure rate of approximately 70%. This is recognized *weakness* due to a number of factors including:

- ✖ Lack of top team commitment.
- ✖ Poorly defined measures or too many measures.
- ✖ Inappropriate milestone goals.
- ✖ Poor deployment in the organization.
- ✖ Obsolete improvement processes.
- ✖ Unrealistic linkage to financial results.

As one survey concluded, the Balanced Scorecard concept appears straightforward but it represents a challenge to most organizations. To quote the study 'it's simple but not easy'. An effective Balanced Scorecard requires the development of complex linkages, which can be difficult to establish. Organizations may also find difficulty in translating the identified linkages into effective operational systems which employees can manage the business with. Development and implementation of a Balanced Scorecard therefore may need to be viewed as a change initiative requiring effective management including:

- Establishing top level commitment.
- Developing a robust design process.
- Creating ownership among employees.
- Managing resistance to change.
- Developing understanding through education and training.
- Agreeing and communicating the measures to be used.

Faced with such challenges many management teams may use less robust development processes, seeking to implement generic high level scorecards with little staff involvement and commitment. This top down approach may focus more on the easier to measure perspectives of finance and process, concentrating on efficiency at the expense of effectiveness. It may also contribute to the already high failure rate. For organizations seeking to utilize the benefits of a Balanced Scorecard, there appears the need to develop practical solutions to the complexity of effectively implementing and operating an apparently compelling concept.

In summary, The Balanced Scorecard presents different challenges. It is a complex and time consuming process. The management and measurement processes needed to be developed in a Balanced Scorecard present substantial barrier to many organizations. A principal benefit from Balanced Scorecard use is as a comprehensive performance management framework which can define and clarify strategy so it is understood by all in the organization and focus senior managers on future performance.

3.2 EFQM Business Excellence Model

The EFQM model was developed in 1991, and revised in 1999, by the European Foundation for Quality Management (EFQM) to help management apply Total Quality Management (TQM) principles. It was originally developed as a quality award framework but its further use as an organizational improvement tool was quickly recognized. This framework is based on nine criteria are split into two categories "Enablers" and "Results". The *Enablers* are the criteria that are concerned with organization whereas the *Results* criteria are concerned with what is being achieved in the organization. In other words, 'Results' are caused by 'Enablers'. The model places as much emphasis on what the organization does and achieve. In addition to the above introduction: [77]

- The EFQM Excellence Model is the most widely used Management Framework in Europe.
- EFQM claim this process of self-assessment provides a systematic learning experience for people within an organization of both excellence concepts and quality improvement. [78]

The main objective of the model is to improve organizational performance through self-assessment and improvement activity against nine major benchmark excellence criteria. In turn, customer results, people results and society results are achieved through leadership driving policy and strategy, people, partnerships and resources and processes, which lead to excellence in key performance results.[79]

---

77   Henrik Andersen, Gavin Lawrie, and Michael Shulver, The Balanced Scorecard vs. The EFQM Business Excellence Model, 6/1/2000, 2GC Active Management, pp. 2-14

78   Members of Quality Scotland, The EFQM Excellence Model & Balanced Scorecard, 2/1/2007, Quality Scotland, pp. 1-4

79   British Quality Foundation (BQF)., The European framework – the EFQM Excellence Model, 1/1/1999, Department of Trade and Industry – UK, pp. 1-3

The enabler criteria of EFQM model are concerned with how the organization approaches "Excellence". The addressed criteria are listed below:

- *Leadership*: How behavior and actions support a culture of "Excellence".
- *Policy and Strategy*: How policy and strategy are formulated and deployed into plans and actions.
- *People*: How the organization realizes the potential of its people.
- *Partnerships and Resources*: How the organization manages resources effectively and efficiently.
- *Processes*: How the organization manages and improves its processes.

The results criteria of EFQM model are concerned with what the organization has achieved. The four results areas are:

- *Customer Results*: What is the customers' perception of the organization and how good are the drivers of customer satisfaction.
- *People Results*: What are the employees' perceptions of the organization and how good are the drivers of employee satisfaction.
- *Society Results*: How does society and the local community perceive the organization and what results have been achieved relating to community and environmental concerns.
- *Key Performance Results*: What is the organization achieving in relation to its planned performance.

Using EFQM model has many clear *benefits*, including:

- ✓ Understanding of overall performance.
- ✓ Creating an opportunity and focus for improvement.
- ✓ Increasing customer and people satisfaction.
- ✓ Improving productivity.

However, according to National Institute of Standards and Technology (NIST), a USA based research; there is little evidence, that these organizational benefits have translated into clear performance improvements. This may in part be due to the difficulty in linking performance improvements directly to EFQM activity. The evidence that does exist is of limited scale and there are doubts over its sustainability. This research did highlight some doubt on such performance improvements. When allowance is made for market and industry factors, the bottom line performance of award winners was 31% below industry benchmarks.[80]

A number of critics explain this lack of compelling evidence of the model's success on its focus on the internal operation of the business. They argue for a 'right to left' use, of the model beginning with the results to be achieved. With such an approach organizations seek to understand firstly what adds value to customers and then adopt a systematic approach to achieve this.

It is also questionable whether the improvements achieved through model use are those needed to achieve sustained future performance. The model lacks a future orientation. It benchmarks the excellence of present day processes. This can create a focus on current performance rather than an assessment of capability for the future. In other words, following the model provides no test of appropriate strategic choice.

A number of issues in using the model can be tracked to its original development as an award framework designed to compare multiple companies. The EFQM model organizational improvement role came later on. The generic content enables a wide application but it can lack relevance for individual

---

80   National Institute of Standards and Technology, who administer the Baldridge
      award

organizations. This may cause problems for some organizations in terms of effective implementation of its strategy. [81]

The difficulty of implementation is a constant theme in the literature. The self assessment approach leaves organizations with a need to define priorities with which to judge the relative merits of intended actions, but the model provides no processes to do so.

The problems of using the generic framework of the model have led to more recent examinations of the benefits of an organizational specific or customized approach. In Europe, 30% of the organizations studied had adjusted the model or developed their own version to reduce resource usage and make the language more relevant to the individual organization.

In summary, use of EFQM appears to improve customer focus and people management through an emphasis on the management of internal processes via effective leadership. The systems approach to an organization may also help managers and staff takes a broader perspective of what constitutes excellent performance. Drawbacks to EFQM use are the terminology in the model; the potential resources required to self-assess an organization and a lack of focus on the specific organizational results to be achieved.

---

81   Steve Johnson, EFQM and Balanced Scorecard - for improving organizational performance, 4/1/2003, Inland Revenue, pp. 8-30

3.3 Activity Based Costing

Activity Based Costing (ABC) is a cost measurement system that provides a cost for each product, service or customer by analyzing each activity needed to produce a product or service to customer. For example, a product that has a short processing cycle may use a disproportionate amount of inventory space or time on the receiving dock. When indirect costs are allocated to a product based on the wrong cost driver, this product will appear less or more expensive than it actually is. ABC is used to identify all activities, direct and indirect, and allocate the costs associated with these activities more precisely.[82]

Activity-based costing addresses deficiencies in the traditional cost accounting systems. These legacy systems are based on a few cost drivers, usually direct labor or direct machine hours, and do not accommodate the recent changes in business environment. As an organization's product and customer mix becomes more diverse, the assignment of overhead expenses becomes grossly misleading, distorting the costs of individual products or services. As a result, many manufacturing organizations have cost systems which can support financial reporting, but provide distorted information about the individual products. This sends the wrong signal to decision makers.

ABC can be used in any type of organization. It is most useful though, when an organization has complex transfer pricing issues, high indirect costs and shared processing stations. ABC provides useful insights, but information without action does not add value. The results should be used to generate improvement. Procter & Gamble makes use of ABC technologies to identify per case cost of inefficient industry practices, and the amounts that can be saved by improving those practices.

---

82   Mark Shinder & David McDowell, ABC, The Balanced Scorecard and EVA - Distinguishing the Means from the End, 4/1/1999, Stern Stewart Europe Limited, pp. 2-7

Process reengineering programs often follow an ABC analysis, with streamlined processes, reduced cost and higher quality pursued.[83]

Many critics argued that ABC system could provide an incomplete picture. While the cost aspect is vital, managers need to understand the impact on revenues, volumes, customer satisfaction, market position, employee morale and a host of other factors. Therefore, cost information alone is insufficient to maximize value. Managers need to understand how costs interact with other performance indicators before they can improve the performance of their business.

83   R. S. Kaplan and R. Cooper; Cost & Effect; Harvard Business School Press, Boston Massachusetts 1998. pp. 197

3.4 Outcomes Based Management

Outcomes Based Management (OBM) has been increasingly implemented by government agencies as part of an inter-related package of financial and administrative reforms. Government agencies are required to identify and report outcomes and key outputs; key outputs defined as discrete goods or services. In OBM, the historical cash-based appropriations regime was replaced by the accrual appropriations regime, which defines an appropriation in terms of the full cost of resources required to deliver specific outputs. Output measures and key indicators of efficiency and effectiveness have been progressively developed to measure agency performance in delivering outputs and achievement of desired outcomes. As the focus has shifted from outputs to outcomes, the framework is now referred to as Outcome Based Management. This name change reflects the fact that government agencies are established and operate with a view to achieving outcomes that are desired by government for the community and should utilize their resources effectively and efficiently to achieve those desired outcomes. Common *weaknesses* that government agencies mistakenly make when using Outcomes Based Management are summarized next.[84]

- ✗ Does not describe well an end result, impact or consequence for the community or target client group.
- ✗ It is not well aligned with the agency's or business unit's mission or purpose.
- ✗ It is not well consistent and not aligned with government's goals.
- ✗ It is not very consistent with enabling legislation.
- ✗ Does not have a strategic focus but focuses on day-to-day activities.

---

84   Department of Treasury and Finance , Outcome Based Management, 11/1/2004, Government of Western Australia, pp. 8-23

✘   Does not describe why an agency delivers particular services, rather than what or how services are delivered.
✘   It is not designed to avoid perverse incentives on staff and managerial behaviors.
✘   It is not well measurable by using potential good KPIs.

3.5 Value Based Management

Value Based Management (VBM) addresses the value of a company which is determined by its discounted future cash flows. Value is created when companies invest capital at returns that exceed the cost of that capital. Value Based Management focuses on how a company uses value to make both major strategic and everyday operating decisions. It is an approach to management that aligns a company's overall goals, analytical techniques, and management processes to focus management decision making on the key drivers of value.[85]

Value Based Management is not a staff-driven exercise. It focuses on better decision making at all levels in an organization. It recognizes that top-down controlled structures cannot work well, especially in large corporations. Instead, it calls on managers to use value-based performance metrics for making better decisions. It entails managing the balance sheet as well as the income statement, and balancing long- and short-term perspectives. When Value Based Management is implemented well, it brings tremendous benefit. It is like restructuring to achieve maximum value on a continuing basis. It could have high impact, often realized in improved economic performance.

Although putting a Value Based Management system in place is a long and complex process, successful efforts share a number of features. As with any major program of organizational change, it is vital for top management to understand and support the implementation. At one company, the CEO and CFO made a video for their employees in which they pledged their support for the initiative, declared that the basis of compensation would shift at the end of the year from earnings to economic profit.

---

85   Timothy Koller, What is value-based management, Vol 3 1994, The Mckinsey Quaterly, pp. 87-100

On one side, adopting a value-based mindset and finding the value drivers gets the organization only halfway. On the other side, managers must establish processes that bring this mindset to life in the daily activities of the company. Line managers could embrace value-based thinking as an improved way of making decisions. For Value Based Management to work properly, it must eventually involve every decision maker in the company. There are four essential management processes that collectively govern the adoption of Value Based Management. These processes are described in the following list:

- A corporate team or business unit develops a strategy to maximize value.
- It translates this strategy into short- and long-term performance targets defined in terms of the key value drivers.
- It develops action plans and budgets to define the steps that will be taken over the next year or so to achieve these targets.
- It puts performance measurement and incentive systems in place to monitor performance against targets and to encourage employees to meet their goals.

First, corporate strategy development is primarily about deciding what businesses to be in, how to exploit potential synergies across business units, and how to allocate resources across businesses. In a Value-Based Management context, senior management devises a corporate strategy that explicitly maximizes the overall value of the company, including buying and selling business units as appropriate. That strategy should be built on a thorough understanding of business-unit strategies. At the business-unit level, strategy development generally entails identifying alternative strategies, valuing them, and choosing the one with the highest value. The chosen strategy should spell out how the business unit will achieve a competitive advantage that will permit it to create value. This explanation should be grounded in a thorough analysis of the market, the competitors, and the unit's assets and skills. The Value-Based Management elements of the strategy then come into play.

Second, once strategies for maximizing value are agreed, they must be translated into specific targets. Target setting is highly subjective, yet its importance cannot be overstated. Targets are the way management communicates what it expects to achieve. Without targets, organizations do not know where to go. Set targets too low, and they may be met, but performance will be mediocre. Set them at unattainable levels, and they will fail to provide any motivation.

Third, action plans translate strategy into the specific steps an organization will take to achieve its targets, particularly in the short term. The plans must identify the actions that the organization will take so that it can pursue its goals in a methodical manner.

Finally, performance measurement and incentive systems track progress in achieving targets and encourage managers and other employees to achieve them. Rarely do front-line supervisors and employees have clear performance measures that are linked to their company's long-term strategy; indeed, many have none at all. Value-Based Management may force a company to modify its traditional approach to performance systems. In particular, it shifts performance measurement from being accounting driven to being management driven. All the same, developing a performance measurement system is relatively straightforward for a company that understands its key value drivers and has set its short- and long-term targets. With regards to compensation design, the first principle in compensation design is that it should provide the incentive to create value at all levels within an organization. Compensation for the chief executive officer is something of a red herring. Managers' performance should be evaluated by a combination of metrics that reflects their organizational responsibilities and control over resources

These four processes are linked across the company at the corporate, business-unit, and functional levels. Clearly, strategies and performance targets must be consistent right through the organization if it is to achieve its value creation goals. Common weaknesses in using Value Based Management are summarized below.

- ✗ Explicit and visible top management support is missing.
- ✗ Little focus among operating personnel on better decision making.
- ✗ Building skills in a wide cross-section of the company is weak.
- ✗ Integration of VBM approach with all elements of planning is not there.
- ✗ Over emphasizing on methodological issues and little focus on practical applications.
- ✗ Use of generic analytical approach that are not tailored to each business unit.
- ✗ Availability of crucial data is not there.
- ✗ Provide un-standardized, difficult-to-use valuation templates and report formats for submission of management reports.
- ✗ Incentives are not tied to value creation.
- ✗ Capital and human resource requests are not linked to value based analysis.

3.6 Economic Value Added

Economic Value Added (EVA) is the one measure that is used to monitor the overall value creation in a business. EVA is not the strategy; it is the way to measure the results. There are many value drivers that need to be managed, but there can be only one measure that demonstrates success. A single measure is needed as the ultimate reference of performance to help managers balance conflicting objectives.

The EVA measure was created by Stern Stewart to address the challenges companies faced in the area of financial performance measurement. By measuring profits after subtracting the expected return to shareholders EVA indicates economic profitability. It tracks share prices much more accurately than earnings, earnings per share, return on equity or other accounting metrics, as strongly supported by practical studies. Creating sustainable improvements in EVA is the same with increasing shareholder wealth.

Stern Stewart & Co. describes Economic Value Added as a "company's net operating profit minus an appropriate charge for the opportunity cost of all capital invested in an enterprise". In equation form, EVA equals net operating profit after taxes, minus the company's book capital, multiplied by its cost of capital. According to Stern Stewart, EVA is an "estimate of a company's true "economic" profit, or the amount by which earnings exceed or fall short of the required minimum rate of return investors could get by investing in other securities of comparable risk."[86]

EVA is not a new concept. Economists have known about the residual income framework for years, but businesses have only recently begun to make the switch from managing for

---

86   Stern Stewart, EVA Metric Wars, 10/1/1996, The Magazine for Senior Financial
       Executives, pp. 1-7

earnings to managing for value. EVA has facilitated this process by providing practical applications that operating managers can use and embrace. When decisions are made, performance is measured and compensation is determined using the same measurement, top management gets accountability. Operating managers also find that EVA simplifies their job, as they barely understand the interaction between the multiple existing measures.

When EVA is the focal point of all management processes, the organization will function more effectively. A common language and a clear objective based on one measure will remove much of the confusion and blurred objectives that cripple organizations. As Dr. Karl-Hermann Baumann, Head of Siemens' supervisory board said "EVA removes the confusion arising from the existence of several planning measures and creates a common language for everyone…for the simple employee and the top manager." A large part of an organization's culture comes from the way success is measured and rewarded. The balanced scorecard can help employees deliver on the corporate vision, but EVA tells them whether they have been successful and should be rewarded. [87]

Although in any given business there are countless individual operating actions that can create value, eventually they must all fall into one of four categories measured by an increase in EVA. Specifically, EVA can be increased through the following four means.

- *Improving the Returns on Existing Capital*: This might be achieved through higher prices or margins, more volume, or lower costs.
- *Profitable Growth*: This might be achieved through investing capital where increased profits will

---

87   Mark Shinder & David McDowell, ABC, The Balanced Scorecard and EVA - Distin-
       guishing the Means from the End, 4/1/1999, Stern Stewart Europe Limited, pp. 2-7

adequately cost of additional capital. Investments in working capital and production capacity may be required to facilitate increased sales, new products or new markets.

- *Harvest*: This might be achieved through rationalizing, liquidating, or curtailing investments in operations that cannot generate returns greater than the cost of capital. This might be through withdrawing from unprofitable markets.

- *Optimize Cost of Capital*: This might be achieved through reducing the cost of capital but maintaining the financial flexibility necessary to support the business strategy through the prudent use of debt, risk management, and other financial products.[88]

---

88   Justin Pettit, EVA and Strategy, 4/1/2000, Stern Stewart Europe Limited, pp. 2-19

CHAPTER 4

STRATEGIC PLAN IMPLEMENTATION

CHAPTER 4: STRATEGIC PLAN IMPLEMENTATION

During the implementation stage, most organizations recognize that there is a significant gap between their strategic plans and their ability to execute this plan. Many organizations top management are dissatisfied in the alignment between strategy and actual results.

Palladium Group identified four main barriers to strategic execution that need to be addressed through an integrated approach. If an organization attacks these barriers, it can improve the judgments that the members of the organization make every day. [89]

- *The Vision Barrier*: In most companies only small part of workforce understands their company's strategy. Even if the employees can recite the company's vision, most have no idea how they personally affect the vision. They do not know where the company is headed or what they can do to help.
- *The People Barrier*: In most companies, employees' personal objectives are not linked to the organization's objectives, creating "The People Barrier" to executing strategy. In fact, few managers have incentives linked to overall strategy. As a result, a selfish mentality takes hold, and individuals focus on the performance of their small group rather than on the success of the entire organization.
- *The Resource Barrier*: When companies do not allocate time, energy, and money to the processes that they have identified as crucial to achieving their strategy, the Resource Barrier occurs. As a result, the energy of

---

89   Lawrence G. Hrebiniak, Organizational Dynamics, "Obstacles to Effective Strategy Implementation" vol. 35, No. 1, 2006

the organization goes to solving short-term problems rather than to achieving strategic objectives.

- *The Management Barrier*: One of the most basic reasons why companies fail to execute their strategy is the lack of management focus. As a result, executive team meetings are unproductive in many organizations, focusing on small projects, short-term objectives, and fighting fires. Strategy is the framework around which all other activity should take place.

In a report prepared by Gartner and Cranfield Business School, the authors found that it is estimated that:

- 5 % of the workforce understands strategy.
- 25 % of managers have incentives linked to strategy.
- 85 % of executives spend less than 1 hour a month in discussing strategy.
- 60 % do not link budgets to strategic plans.

The report goes on to say that a tool is needed which contains both short- and long-term measures, as well as financial and non-financial ones. The tool must be acceptable to all sectors of the workforce; easily understood and communicate overall business strategy; must show the drivers necessary for long-term results and indicate every employee's contribution to overall success; easy to use; integrate with existing business systems; and must fit in with the overall culture of the organization.

Companies that use a balanced set of strategic measures, both financial and non-financial, outperform their less disciplined rivals in performance and management. A recent national survey of 203 executives on measurement found that not many companies report being "measurement managed," with clearly defined and updated measures in place for assessing employees, suppliers and customers as well as key attributes such as levels of adaptability and innovativeness. Until recently, with the exception of financial results, measurement has not exactly been a burning issue for top management. Common *weaknesses* that could happen during strategy implementation are summarized below. [90]

- ✗ The strategy is not worth implementing.
- ✗ People are not clear how the strategy will be implemented.
- ✗ Customers and staff do not fully understand the strategy.
- ✗ Individual responsibilities for implementing the change are not clear.
- ✗ Senior managers step out of the picture once implementation begins.
- ✗ No dedicated internal unit to handle and track strategic planning process.
- ✗ Usage of confusing terminology in the strategic plans.
- ✗ Over-engineered strategic plans which are complex to understand.
- ✗ Lack of communication and confidentiality issues.
- ✗ Lack of leadership involvement in the strategic planning process.
- ✗ Individual work often undercuts organizational achievement.
- ✗ Some work is irrelevant to strategic goals.
- ✗ Strategic goals unsupported by enough tactical results.
- ✗ Work overlaps and redundancies that lead to conflicts and waste.
- ✗ Unrealistic objectives that can't be translated onto real action plans.
- ✗ Employees achieve much activities and effort but little end results.

The most important and critical items on the strategy execution check list are designed to address the content, process, and

---

90   William Schiemann & John Lingle, Seven Greatest Myths Of Measurement, Metrus Group, 2-4

impact of moving the strategic plan to operations during implementation phase. The recommended *check list* items are listed next:

- ✓ There is a formal link between strategic initiatives defined and established process management programs (i.e. TQM, Six Sigma).
- ✓ There is a clear allocation of budgets for strategic initiatives.
- ✓ Strategic targets can be easily associated with operational targets.
- ✓ Strategy has been mapped effectively onto existing processes to identify gaps.
- ✓ The overall management of initiatives across the organization delivering anticipated benefits and outcomes.
- ✓ Various elements of strategy are practical and applicable (i.e. target and measures) in the implementation of the strategy.
- ✓ The strategy provides an effective way of managing initiatives with realizable benefits.
- ✓ Increase the awareness of the importance of employees to spend more time in analyzing local issues.
- ✓ Strategy mapped onto day-to-day processes with emphasis on the contribution of operation to the strategy.
- ✓ Flexibility should be in financial plans due to possible need of immediate funding for things with significant impact on the business.
- ✓ Information should be easily accessed by putting more emphasis on transparency.
- ✓ Learning curve of employees needs to be taken into consideration.
- ✓ Having continuous evaluation of the situation.
- ✓ Recognition should be more than once a year and that will increase the loyalty and motivation.

- ✓ Clear, unambiguous relationships between goals, objectives, measures and initiatives.
- ✓ Use of specific measures and initiatives by management to improve commitment and buy-in from staff.
- ✓ Appraisal system linked to a bonus component.
- ✓ Verifying the efficiency of the vendor in delivering required outsourced and critical services.
- ✓ Adaptation level of external consultants to the nature of the organization, the culture, and the region.
- ✓ Track objectives with good financial and non-financial measures.
- ✓ Implement strategy management methodology that is supported by a good IT system.
- ✓ Continuity in leadership sponsorship and commitment.
- ✓ Defined owner for each initiative.

4.1 Internal Organizational Capability

With regards to strategic plan execution inside an organization, three main institutional capability requirements have been identified. These critical capabilities are human resource skills, internal processes, and information technology. Each of the three institutional capabilities is responsible for contributing to an effective and successful implementation of the organization strategic plan. Some of the major concerns that will have an impact on the implementation process, and will need to be resolved are; changes required within the organization; technical skills requirements; information sharing; and technology platforms required to facilitate strategy implementation.

With regards to human resource capabilities, many studies signaled that there were several recurring issues relevant to effective implementation of the strategic plans. The *recommendations* are highlighted below:

- ✓ Making sure that the employees who will execute the strategic plan have the technical abilities and capacity to do so.
- ✓ Sharing information within and across divisions to identify internal and external concerns.
- ✓ System in place which will facilitate the development of employees through coaching and mentoring techniques.
- ✓ Employee compensation system that rewards superior achievements through pay and incentives.
- ✓ Development of employees through training and education initiatives.
- ✓ Building internal human resource capacity to achieve the strategic plan.
- ✓ Mechanism in place to identify poor performance and advice on disciplinary action.

- ✓ Cascading enough empowerment, authority, and responsibility to staff.
- ✓ Foster a commitment-oriented change mindset as opposed to it being compliance-driven.

In relation to internal process capabilities, there were several common issues relevant to the effective implementation of the strategic plans. The findings and *recommendations* are highlighted below:

- ✓ Integrated business process with clear linkage between the business plans and financial processes.
- ✓ Mitigate the overlap in mandates between departments with clarity of purpose.
- ✓ Clear delineation of roles and responsibilities with accompanying decentralization and accountability to ensure effective implementation of the strategic plan.
- ✓ Funds need to be clearly earmarked for building process capability.
- ✓ Clear internal policy and procedures framework to avoid ambiguity in the implementation of the strategic plan.
- ✓ Promote a culture of process innovation.

In regards to information technology capabilities, there were several recurring issues that are relevant to effective implementation of the strategic plans. The findings and *recommendations* are highlighted below:

- ✓ Have access to reliable and accurate data to assist with the implementation of the strategic plan.
- ✓ Use of IT in delivering services to final customers.
- ✓ The need for compliance with government standards when developing IT systems.
- ✓ Effective integration of systems within the same organization.

- ✓ Effective integration of systems with major stakeholders and suppliers.
- ✓ Ability to communicate and relay information between networks.
- ✓ Availability of internal applications to meet the organization needs.
- ✓ Making sure the internal and external IT platform is regularly updated by keeping up with new technologies.
- ✓ The implementation of an advanced employee performance management system.

Additional ideas to help solve internal organization issues include the following *action list* items:

- ✓ As part of the strategic planning process, establish a working group composed of departmental representatives to assist the process and an executive committee to oversees, reviews, and provides input on the various stages of the strategic planning process.
- ✓ Ensure that finance department is part of the internal planning process so that budgeting is not made more difficult and disconnected from the strategic planning process.
- ✓ Provide a strategic planning framework that is available from the outset and which can be adapted to meet the organization needs.
- ✓ Simplify the strategic planning manual to use clearer terminology and become less process-centric.

4.2 Communication and Education

In today's highly dynamic business environment strategy has never been more important. To succeed, organizations need to continuously reshape themselves. This requires tremendous leadership and strategic agility as well as superior execution of the chosen strategy. Organizations that fail to engage their people to strategy execution fail to achieve their full potential. Organizational success requires that employees are truly engaged and committed to their work and share the values and goals of the organization.[91]

Intuition tells us that when employees are truly engaged in their work and in the values and goals of the organization, their behavior will generally support organizational success. It seems equally self-evident that disengaged employees are unlikely to give their best. In order to confirm this intuition several studies have been conducted. Research indeed indicates that engaged employees are more loyal. The greater the number of more loyal employees, the lower the costs of recruiting, hiring, training, and developing, not to mention the positive effects on productivity. Engaged employees are also more willing to give extra effort when the organization needs it.

The organization has to be educated. To accomplish this they will establish comprehensive programs to communicate to the organization what's important. Best practice companies have found ways to use the complete spectrum of communication techniques such as town hall meetings, newsletters, personal appearances, open door policies, and web conversations. Finally, the organization has to measure of how staff's understand the strategy.

---

91   Balanced Scorecard Collaborative, QPR ScoreCard, 1/1/2004, QPR Software Plc

According to a research conducted by W. Schiemann & Associates Inc, when managers were asked how well their business strategy was communicated and understood from top to bottom at their organizations, the result was 60% of managers rated favorably how well the strategy was communicated throughout the organization. Good communication demands a clear message. If the strategy itself is unclear, insisting on measures for strategic goals can force clarity, as it has at Sears. Sears senior executives said "There was a real gap between the strategy and what it meant on a day-to-day, operational basis" This left employees uncertain about how they could contribute. Sears senior executives added a number of communication elements to the strategy and then tied the key strategic goals to performance measures. This helped to clarify the strategic thinking and bring to life what Sears wants to become and how to get there. Measurement also provides a common language for communication. People talk about how they're being measured. It is almost the language in which communication occurs in an organization. Consistent with the notion of a common language, in the above research 71% of managers reported that information within their organization was shared openly and honestly.[92]

Another study published in the "Journal of Strategic Communication Management" analyzed organizational performance based on how well the strategy was communicated to employees. The results are summarized in the following two groups:[93]

- In well-performing organizations
  - 67% of employees have a good understanding of overall organizational goals.

---

[92]   John H. Lingle, From BSC to IS Measurement, 1/1/2007, Wm. Schiemann & Associates Inc, 1-6

[93]   Robert S. Kaplan, Communication and Education to Make Strategy Everyone's Job, 6/22/2005, Harvard Business Review, pp. 3-6

- ○   26% of senior managers are highly effective communicators.

- •   In Poorly-performing organizations
  - ○   38% of employees have a good understanding of overall organizational goals.
  - ○   0% of senior managers are highly effective communicators.

Fonvielle and Carr argued that when alignment is strong, employees and management work to accomplish same goal, motivation and energy becomes high, and both individual and team contribution increase. At the beginning, alignment is usually strong at small start-up companies where few people focus on few critical business goals. These companies are characterized by strong sense of dedication with high personal engagement. Commitment is reflected in long workdays and personal sacrifices for the good of the team. Usually, the challenge is to keep this alignment strong as the firm grows in size and complexity. In turn, alignment is essential for successful implementation of strategy.[94]

Top managers often comment that getting their employees aligned with the company's strategy is their most important and one of their most challenging tasks. Dr. Bob Frost, director of a consulting firm called Measurement International, acknowledges the challenges of the alignment process. He highlighted once that when alignment within a company is weak, people end up working for different purposes, and actions become less effective. He added that most common dilemma is when functional or individual objectives take priority over the company or customer objective. Productivity and ethics diminish over time, and the company becomes more at risk to competitors and market forces. Common *weaknesses* that could

---

94   William Fonvielle and Lawrence P. Carr, Gaining Alignment - Making Scorecards Work, 1/3/1999, Management Accounting, pp. 1-12

negatively affect communication and its channels are described next:.

- ✗ Individuals have different goals in mind but have unstated disagreements.
- ✗ Uncommitted group exist within the organization, ensuring that overall commitment to any chosen strategy is fragile.
- ✗ Many members are unconvinced of the proposed action.
- ✗ Employees don't know what the goals of the organization are.

Today, objective setting process exists in a challenging environment. It is a top-down cascading process. Staff found out what the boss's objectives were. From those objectives, this employee figured out what his/her little piece of those objectives was. Now, it was found that if every person in the organization is exposed to the entire strategy, that individuals will find areas that they can contribute to that are totally outside of their traditional job scope.

A survey of 293 organizations in the United Kingdom showed that in poorly performing organizations, 66% of employees did not have a good understanding of overall organization goals. Even in well-performing organizations, approximately 33% did not understand the organization's goals. Many media tools are available to communicate the strategy to employees including:[95]

- *Brochures*: A brief document that describes strategic objectives and how these will be measured can be issued at the beginning of the strategy implementation.
- *Monthly Newsletters*: The first issues of the newsletter define and describe strategy. Subsequent issues report

---

95   Robert S. Kaplan, Communication and Education to Make Strategy Everyone's Job, 6/22/2005, Harvard Business Review, pp. 3-6

on the measures and feature stories about employee initiatives that are actually improving performance.

- *Education Programs*: Incorporating the strategy in all education and training programs reinforces the message that following the organization strategy is the way of doing business.
- *Quarterly Meetings*: Initially, executives use quarterly town meetings to introduce the strategy. As the concept becomes established, executives use them to brief employees on performance and to engage in question-and-answer discussions about the future.
- *Company Intranet*: Strategy is posted on the intranet, complete with audio and video segments of executives describing the overall strategy and explaining objectives, measures, targets, and initiatives.

Perhaps it is important to mention that there are privacy concerns and risks in sharing a strategy details with hundreds and thousands of employees. Employees come and go, and not everyone is fully aligned to the company's values, mission, and sustained success. In one case example, company lawyers stopped the project team at one company from communicating strategy to all employees. They feared the possible public disclosure of the financial data and other projections contained in the strategy, which would have violated securities law. This objection stopped the deployment of the strategy for months. Only after this company fortified its intranet, by building in two levels of access security, was the strategy details released. The executive leadership team could access the actual numbers on the vertical scale for the measures; all other employees could only see the trends against the target. Companies may want to follow this example to avoid the risk of disclosing sensitive information to competitors or the public.[96]

---

96   R. Kaplan, Communication and Education to Make Strategy Everyone's Job, 6/22/2005, Harvard Business Review.

As part of communication plan, strategy implementation team could conduct communication sessions and must be able to:

- Drive and facilitate strategic dialogue.
- Detect personal and political agendas.
- Highlight the big picture of the business.
- Synthesize data and information.
- Address questions that may not be politically correct.
- Detect executive leadership champions and allies.
- Act on the best interests of the business as a whole.
- Capture feedback from employees and all stakeholders.

Effective communication helps every employee understand the strategy, which helps them align their conduct to the strategy. Main *benefits* and purpose of communication plan are described in the following list:

- ✓ Fostering personal commitment to strategy implementation.
- ✓ A performance focused structure and program.
- ✓ Shared purpose and clear accountability.
- ✓ Optimized enterprise, not merely optimized business units.
- ✓ Higher employee satisfaction.
- ✓ Commitment from the organization to execute the strategy.
- ✓ Provide feedback on the strategy and direction.
- ✓ Education to the organization about the strategy.

Communication is not enough to ensure strategic alignment. It is the job of all employees to find ways to help the company meet its strategic goals. By aligning performance management and evaluation with the company's strategy, organizations can assure that employees' actions are helping to achieve the strategy.

Effective communication is essential to developing strategic awareness in an enterprise. Without it, people will either understand how they relate to the strategy incorrectly, or not understand it at all. Potential *consequences* of not communicating enough to employees include the following issues:

- ✘ People may not understand how they relate to the strategy, and may not effectively support it.
- ✘ Interest may decrease, causing morale to drop, and talent is difficult to retain.
- ✘ Money may be wasted on programs that don't support strategy.
- ✘ Organization is not strategy-focused.

Executives must lead strategy communication, than manage the processes and tools to facilitate ongoing communication. There are three types of communication which occur from the earliest stages of a communication plan and continue through implementation and beyond. The three types of communication are: marketing, information, and feedback. All three types of strategy communication are necessary to communicate the strategy to an organization effectively. The three types of communication need to be integrated into a unified plan for communication. It is important to note that communication in this context does not only mean one-way communication from the management team to employees, but also how management accepts feedback, learning, and comments from the workforce.

Accountability for implementation should be given to someone who has experience successfully rolling out corporate-wide communications of a strategic nature. The following six points roughly translate into the activities that are necessary to create a communication plan.

- Communication plan owner.
- Communication program objectives.
- Audiences.
- Message and the Messenger (speaker).
- Media.
- Frequency.

It is worth mentioning that there are external people with whom top management may choose to share the plan with, such as parent organization, customers, suppliers, stakeholders. If top management wants to share the plan externally, it needs to be clear about its desired outcomes. The level of detail provided may be different from what is needed for an internal audience. Following are *reasons* to share the plan with various external organizations:

- ✓ Improve relations with customers by demonstrating a focus on their needs.
- ✓ Gain support of other organizations that may be able to help the organization save resources and achieve common goals.
- ✓ Gain parent organization's support and justify additional resources.
- ✓ Emphasize supplier's roles in doing business with the organization.
- ✓ Align stakeholders with the vision.
- ✓ Gain union leaders' acceptance and positive participation.

After the strategic plan is formally deployed, top management must be prepared to answer questions and face skepticism and challenges. Staff will realize that implementation of the strategic plan means that real change will take place and that the organization will go through a period of transition, meaning that initially people may need to find time to take on additional work. Many organizations have not legitimized and practiced planning for the future as a regular part of the top management's daily work; nor do they consider implementation as a regular part of the staff work. However, the old work must still be done while new work processes and methods are being developed.

Usually, when an employee is faced with change, many act by denying, resisting, exploring, and then committing to the change. Employees may go through these four stages of change at their own pace. Some may never accept new roles and methods. Often these employees leave the organization. Top management needs to acknowledge and legitimize these stages by preparing a detailed action plan.

The most important and critical items on the strategy communication check list are designed to address the content, process, and impact of communicating on strategic plan implementation. The recommended *check list* items are as follows:

- ✓ Create an internal communications department to assume all contact with stakeholders.
- ✓ Management focuses its communication messages to drive buy-in.
- ✓ Conduct awareness sessions prior to the commencement of the strategic planning exercise.
- ✓ Undertake informal communication workshops to develop plans and eliminate any overlap between stakeholders.
- ✓ Internal strategic planning unit will facilitate interaction between stakeholders.

4.3 Performance Monitoring and Evaluation

Once the strategy has been planned and linked to a comprehensive operational plan, the company begins to execute its strategic and operational plans, monitor the performance results, and act to improve operations and strategy based on new information and learning.

It is possible for organization to execute their strategies but, without a strong performance management model underpinning these strategies, it would be impossible for each organization to assess how well it is closing the gap identified by its strategic goals. It is a structured approach of evaluating corporate performance within a broader strategy execution framework and, through its results; the organization can adapt its strategy and resource allocation accordingly to ensure it meets stated targets.

Ongoing communication of performance results is crucial for success. It is extremely important for top management to share lessons learned, to share successes, and to show that work is being accomplished. The fact that senior leaders are paying attention to goal accomplishment will focus everyone's attention on the plan.

Performance reporting is where organization begins to put the communication to work. Performance reporting provides insight into how well the organization is doing in executing the strategy usually laid out on the strategy map. Performance reporting process provides a framework for reviewing the measures that support strategic objectives. When measures are off target, reporting enables the organization to review and adjust the initiatives that support strategic objectives.

Performance report is the document the organization creates in preparation for reporting meeting, which use to monitor progress in executing the strategy. The ultimate goal of the performance report is to generate discussion, make course corrections, and determine the next steps in the implementation of the strategy. Performance report contains:

- A visual overview in the form of the strategy of how the organization is performing.
- A performance analysis, with an objective owner identified for each strategic objective.
- Measure details, including measure owners, calculation methods, and actual figures as compared to established targets. Charts and graphs are often used.
- Initiative details, including accountability, milestones, completion status, and progress comments.

Preparation of the report includes key organizational analysis required to accurately represent performance to strategy. Preparation of the report generally contains four distinct activities:

- *Collect Data*: There are several sources from which organizations pull data to populate the performance report. Some are easily accessible, while some are more difficult to locate and access. As time progresses, the organization will generally streamline the process.
- *Conduct Analysis*: The process of regularly gathering, organizing, and studying information in the effort to determine how well the organization has achieved the objectives defined in its strategy. Strategic performance analysis focuses on the performance of the organization as an entity and not on the performance of individuals. Performance analysis tests the soundness of organization's strategy; it determines whether the hypotheses about how to achieve the vision and mission are correct.
- *Determine Performance Status*: Determination of Red/Yellow/Green status should be based on

organizationally accepted standard definitions. In general Green means that the team is satisfied with the current level of performance and expects it to continue. Yellow means the current performance falls short of expectations, but progress is being made. Red means the current performance falls short and requires initiatives and resources to drive improvement.

- *Summarize, Synthesize Data and Compile Report*: Is especially critical in normalizing the report for the organization. The analyst must objectively review the status applied to all objectives, measures, and initiatives, and determine if they accurately reflect "reality" and the performance against the strategy.

At operational review meetings, companies examine departmental and functional performance and address problems and issues. Organizations conduct strategy review meetings to discuss the indicators and initiatives from the business unit's plans and assess the progress and barriers to strategy execution. By holding separate operational and strategy review meetings, companies avoid having short-term operational and tactical issues displace discussions of strategy implementation and adaptation. [97]

Operational review meetings characterized of the following activities:

- Examine short-term performance and respond to newly identified problems that need immediate attention.
- Correspond to the frequency with which operational data are generated and the speed at which management wants to respond to sales and operating

---

97   D. P. Norton and J. R. Weiser, "The Strategy Review Process," BSR November–December 2006

data and the numerous other tactical issues that continually emerge.
- Could be weekly, bi-weekly, or even daily meetings to review operating dashboards of sales, bookings, and shipments and to solve such short-term problems as complaints from important customers, late deliveries, a near term cash shortfall, or a new sales opportunity.
- Are typically departmental and function-based, bringing together the expertise and experience of employees to solve day-to- day issues in such areas as sales, purchasing, logistics, finance, and operations. These meetings should be short, highly focused, data-driven, and action oriented.

Strategy review meetings characterized of the following activities:

- Scheduled once a month or quarter to bring together the CEO and executive committee members to review the progress of the strategy.
- Discuss whether strategy execution is on track.
- Track the source and causes of implementation problems.
- Recommend corrective actions.
- Assign responsibility for achieving the targeted performance.
- Are the "check" and "act" portions of strategy execution through the path of the plan-do-check-act (PDCA) cycle

Conducting strategic review meetings generally contains three distinct steps:

- *Pre-brief all Stakeholders*: It is important to pre-brief members of the leadership team prior to the strategy review meeting to ensure that personal and political agendas do not interfere with the strategy discussion, and to set the approach for the meeting.

- *Manage Logistics*: Meeting logistics such as date and time, participants list, location, agenda, equipment and facilities required some preparation. It is very important that all leadership team members have the meeting firmly embedded in their calendars.
- *Conduct the Meeting*: Focus discussion on causal relationships among elements of the strategy, and on strategy as a whole, not on the failings of one particular unit.

Because in-depth discussion of every objective, measure, and initiative would require too much time at each monthly meeting, many companies now organize their strategy review meetings by strategic themes, covering one or two in depth at each meeting. Theme owners circulate performance report data on measures and initiatives in advance of the meeting so executives can come prepared with ideas and solutions. The meeting time focuses on action plans for new issues. Meetings could also allow time for urgent issues that cannot wait for the next meeting to be dealt with. Each objective is thus examined carefully at least once per quarter. [98]

With regards to analyzing performance variation, it allows management to analyze target vs. actual variation. The key question for management is whether the variation is random and inherent in the design of the process or whether forces outside the design of the process are causing the variation. Management must respond to common cause variation and special cause variation in distinct ways. Confusing the two, or not being able to distinguish between them, can cause serious and costly mistakes.[99]

---

98   Dr. Robert Kaplan & David Norton, Integrated Strategy Planning and Operational Execution A Six-Stage System, 6/1/2008, Balanced Scorecard Report, pp. 2-6

99   Larry B. Weinstein and Joseph F. Castellano, Scorecard Support, pp. 1-5

In the research conducted by W. Schiemann & Associates Inc. to understand how executives see the "value" and "quality" of information of the following six strategic performance areas, the outcomes are listed in Table 3.

Table 3: Information value and quality for strategic performance areas

Performance Area	Highly Valuable Info.	Quality info.
Financial performance	82%	61%
Operating efficiency	79%	41%
Customer satisfaction	85%.	29%
Employee performance	67%	16%
Innovation/change	52%	16%
Community/environmental	53%	25%

Source: W. Schiemann & Associates Inc

The above research samples these two questions:

- How highly do you value information in each strategic performance area?
- Would you bet your job on the quality of information in each of the areas?

By looking closely to the above survey results they concluded that information about customer satisfaction is highly valued by the largest percentage of executives, even more than financial performance and operating efficiency. In today's competitive marketplace, knowledge about customers is a strong competitive advantage. 67% of executives place a high level of importance on employee performance, and nearly half of all managers place importance on innovation/change and community/environment.

Also, the level of confidence of executives about quality of information varied among each strategic area. In the area of financial performance, only six-in-10 executives place confidence in the data that is available to them. There exists a wide gap between what is valued and what is treated as accurate. Executives face an urgent task of re-examining their measurement system to gain greater self-knowledge and self-confidence. Executives feel so uncertain about the quality of information concerning customers, employees, innovation, change and other external stakeholders such as community groups. Survey findings point to two factors that contribute to executive uncertainty: the clarity of measures in each strategic area of the business, and the frequency with which measurement is undertaken. [100]

After evaluation process, strategy refinement should occur, on average, once a year where a complete review of entity strategies is carried out to ensure that changes in the external environment are factored into a revision of these strategies. This is to ensure that organization strategies continue to be in line with the changing dynamic external environment. Such a review should be conducted in line with the existing strategy framework; any of which may also be reviewed in line with potential changes in the external environment.

If an organization's strategy contains significant flaws, or has become obsolete due to changes in the external environment, the organization should revert to the strategy development process to develop a new transformational strategy. However, if the strategy and its underlying assumptions are still valid, the output of strategy refinement would merely serve to re-affirm the existing strategy, in which case senior management would only need to update targets, re-prioritize strategic initiatives and transmit new expectations to business units and functions. In the situation where neither a drastic renewal of strategy nor its re-affirmation is necessary, incremental changes to strategy can be made by changing one or more measures with new ones or adjusting the strategy's targets and initiatives.

---

100   John H. Lingle, From BSC to IS Measurement, 1/1/2007, Wm. Schiemann & Associates Inc.

The important and critical items on the performance evaluation and monitoring check list are designed to address the content, process, and impact of performance monitoring during evaluation phase. The recommended items are described in the following *check list*:

- ✓ A well-developed and effective performance management and monitoring framework to support execution of the strategy.
- ✓ Sufficient tools and processes available to monitor progress in strategy execution.
- ✓ Strategy team to facilitate and monitor the strategy implementation.
- ✓ Strategic objectives have been identified during strategy review meetings, and resources have been allocated to managing them.
- ✓ Decisions are being made effectively, following performance reviews, to re-shape and re-priorities the strategy implementation or re-allocate resources across the organization.
- ✓ Reviews of the strategy are carried out periodically and effectively.
- ✓ Key performance evaluation and monitoring processes formally identified and documented.

After strategy evaluation stage, strategy refinement becomes important to do. The following check list is designed to address the content, process, and of performance monitoring on re-evaluating and adjusting the strategy for next cycle. The recommended items are described in the following *check list*:

- ✓ There are adequate structured procedures in place to sustain a continuous strategy development and implementation process.

✓ The strategy development framework enables rapid incorporation of new issues and strategic challenges (internal and external) to refine the strategy.

✓ The strategy implementation process is adaptable to take into account new changes to corporate strategy.

✓ There is a feeling of re-assurance that there is a structured and well-developed process to manage strategy going forward.

✓ The organization has developed a culture of learning from previous results.

✓ The organization factors learning into the strategy refinement process.

✓ Evaluation of strategy implementation feeds back into strategy development.

✓ An effective governance process in place within the organization to help react effectively to any changes in the environment and therefore re-prioritization of strategy objectives.

✓ Strategy development framework enables rapid incorporation of new issues and strategic challenges.

✓ Need to be flexible in adjusting procedures and processes of the organization.

✓ Management must ensure that changes from above are absorbed throughout the organization.

✓ Fewer changes to the strategic plan help in execution phase.

✓ Clear to see the strategic contribution of processes being refined or re-engineered for improved alignment to the strategy.

4.4 Rewards and Recognition Programs

Incentives and rewards are important piece of making strategy everyone's job. Incentive compensation helps organizations move beyond creating strategic awareness to motivate people to behave strategically. What most organizations have found is that compensation makes people pay attention. They want the strategy to work. They look at the measures and objectives because they are interested. But, when the organization ties it to their compensation, people usually pay attention.

In turn, innovative new programs for building incentive compensation programs for creating balanced paychecks have started to emerge. Many organizations begin designing and implementing incentive compensation programs during their strategy implementation. A variety of approaches have been used by organizations to tie financial incentives to strategic performance, such as:[101]

- The percentage of total compensation subject to an incentive plan can be small (5%) or substantial (60% or more).
- Base salaries % increase is used to reward employees for the successful achievement of their day-day roles and responsibilities.
- The target level of the annual incentive % could be established. The employee may earn 0% to 150% of the target annual incentive based on the achievement of certain company financial measures and individual performance objectives.
- Some governmental organizations have even found ways to use discretionary funding to encourage strategic performance.

101   Bob Paladino, Integrating Balanced Scorecards with Human Capital Compensation - Rewards and Recognition Programs to Drive Value, Balanced Scorecard
Collaborative, pp. 1-7

- Special recognition program that recognizes employees real-time for performance that may not be captured as part of the individual performance management process. Employees nominate either teams or individuals quarterly for consideration of awards.

In their journeys to become strategy focused, most organizations intend to tie incentive compensation to strategy. Those that have already linked incentive compensation to strategic performance say that if they could do it over again, they would implement these programs sooner. An indication of the impact such programs typically have. It is important to consider the design issues that can most influence performance, including: [102]

- How quickly the program is implemented.
- The use of quantitative versus qualitative measures.
- The number of measures tied to compensation decisions.
- Whether to reward individual, team behavior, or combination of both.
- How often to update these reward systems.
- How to effectively prototype them as a way of getting started.

Organizations today can overcome the people obstacle by linking employees to organizational objectives. Many companies have developed several integrated programs to reinforce employee behaviors to drive strategic objectives by rewarding such behaviors. Erik Agostoni, director of Human Capital Compensation & Benefits at CCI, indicates there are

---

102   David P. Norton and Randall H. Russell,, Motivate to Make Strategy Everyone's Job, 12/1/2004, Balanced Scorecard Report, pp. 2-5

two key steps in developing integrated programs that help to overcome the people obstacle:[103]

- Setting expectations around the roles and responsibilities of positions to ensure strategic objectives are met.
- Linking position roles and responsibilities to compensation elements in an overall competitive total rewards program.

In short, successfully creating a reward and recognition system relies on a stable, well communicated, and well-supported strategy. Otherwise, morale will fall fast as the workforce feels itself striving for a moving target, or being punished for not achieving something that they do not understand or do not have the tools to achieve.

An organization's existing compensation plan may or may not be compatible with its new strategy. For example, the current plan may be tied to behavior that is not easily measured, or may not match the spirit of the new strategy. The organization may need to consider changing the system, given the risks and rewards that come with such a change. A compensation and reward system can become a great asset if the system rewards people for strategic work. It can also be a liability if the system rewards counter-productive behavior, or moves employees' focus away from what supports the strategy.

Tying strategy to compensation is a critical step in implementation. Nonetheless, an organization should not rush to do it too soon. If the organization has not implemented initiatives critical to success, employees can become frustrated and demoralized when targets are not met or payout is not

---

103   B. Paladino, Integrating Balanced Scorecards with Human Capital Compensa-
       tion - Rewards and Recognition Programs to Drive Value, Balanced Scorecard
       Collaborative.

achieved. They need to have a fixed target, and know that they have the tools they need to meet that target.

Most organizations wait one to two years to begin tying their strategy to compensation. In the interim, some organizations use non-cash rewards to provide focus and recognition for achievement. Non-cash recognition is a powerful tool to recognize individual performance and to provide motivation to employees. Non-cash recognition can be made a part of total reward system. The following times and cases are when non-cash rewards could be appropriate:

- Transition strategy for implementing cash compensation plan.
- Reward vehicle for broad organizational reward to integrate with the communications plan and strategy.
- Reward for short term emphasis on projects, initiatives, or critical milestones.
- Reward measurable behaviors necessary to achieve goals.

Linking reward and recognition to strategy helps alleviate many problems. Reward and recognition are based on performance to strategy. Employee attention and focus on reward is undoubtedly sensitive, but exercising it too soon can produce many un-intended side effects. For one thing the measures linking the strategy to compensation may be unproven and lead to dysfunctional decision-making on the part of managers looking to cash in. Targets are also an issue, especially for new measures. An aggressive target may be perceived as unattainable and unrealistic causing employees to lose any motivation they may have had to achieve it. On the other hand, a target easily achieved will do little to foster breakthrough performance. Should the compensation link come under fire, employees, managers, and executives alike may be quick in assigning blame to an inherent shortcoming of the strategy itself rather than properly taking the responsibility for an ill-conceived compensation scheme. Reward and recognition common *weaknesses* are described below.

- ✗ Poor communications of reward and recognition programs.
- ✗ Objectives and goals are unclear.
- ✗ Management unaware of what's available.
- ✗ Rewarding the wrong behaviors.
- ✗ Little or no employee involvement.
- ✗ Disconnects between employees & management goals and needs.
- ✗ Too much money spent without clear understanding of return on investment.

The important and critical items on the reward and recognition check list are designed to address the content, process, and impact of reward and recognition during strategy execution phase. The recommended items are described in the following *check list*:

- ✓ Reward model that includes professional development, and motivating career plan.
- ✓ Ownership of all employees in strategy execution.
- ✓ Implementation of individual performance model to connect the individual performance with the organizational performance, and in turn to strategy.
- ✓ Focus on relationships between staff competency and staff deliverables to strategy.
- ✓ Have to ensure that the organization as a whole understands key processes.
- ✓ Conduct process mapping and process re-engineering activities.
- ✓ Promote achievements through awareness and education.

4.5 Leadership, Ownership and Responsibility

If an organization is expecting to execute strategy well, it must drive behavioral changes within the organization. Building a strong team of leaders to communicate and champion the strategic plan is essential. This issue could be one of the most challenging tasks. Managers' commitment and leadership levels and the roles that they can play are essential for successful implementation of the strategic plan. Leadership entails the ability to surface the need for change; to suppress or remove barriers to change; and to secure short-term wins. These three objectives are done by:

- ✓ Not suppressing internal conflict to enable key players to see the need for change.
- ✓ Closely monitor corporate noise levels. Corporate noise occurs when different parts of an organization are unable to resolve alignment issues between themselves and instead continually escalate these issues to senior management for resolution.
- ✓ Facilitating realization of the need for change using influencing skills.
- ✓ Being ready to present a plan of action for change quickly.
- ✓ Effecting a major, highly visible action aimed at creating a sense of oneness/unity.
- ✓ Establishing ways for easier communication/ interaction between disparate groups.
- ✓ Continually promoting a sense of corporate ownership.
- ✓ Engendering strong buy-in by seeing through promised actions.
- ✓ Identify and quickly implement high value-adding initiatives with short delivery timeframes to communicate intent and delivery focus.
- ✓ Display strong energy and authority.

In addition, the need for a corporate support team is very important. The general purpose of this corporate team is to foster synergies among the various business units and support units. Corporate team must find ways to enable these synergies among the business and support units. Based on strategic direction, corporate team might consider:

- Reallocation of capital to strategic functions.
- Enable resource sharing to create economies of scale.
- Enable and encourage customer sharing to cross-sell products.
- Support and fund knowledge sharing and best practices among business units.
- Encourage and reward behaviors that support strategy.

Strong corporate strategy team is critical to the success of the strategy implementation. A good team combines strategic vision with advocacy, communication and administrative skills to keep the process on track and aligned with the corporate strategy. The number of employees assigned to corporate strategy team on a full-time basis can vary by organization. However, it can range between 3 and 15 personnel, with the average of 7 employees.

The corporate strategy team might also be referred to as a "change agent" for executive leadership. This role works behind the scenes in many cases as a missionary, a consultant, a point person, and a chief of staff, to shepherd the strategy from the earliest development stage to sustainable execution stage. This central role of corporate strategy team is mainly to:

- Provide an integrated approach to strategy management that bridges traditional functional domains such as finance, planning, and performance measurement.

- Ensures that the organization sustains its focus on strategy by integrating strategic focus concepts and principles into the organization.
- Focus on integration of governance systems for strategy.

The corporate strategy team is primarily responsible for oversight and administration of strategy execution. Managing strategy is different than managing functions:

- Traditional competencies are based on functional niches which create silos.
- Strategic management requires cross-functional processes.
- There is no logical home for cross-functional processes.

In general, the corporate strategy team is the custodian of cross-business processes required to execute strategy. The corporate strategy team owns or coordinates the following steps in the strategy planning cycle:

- *Strategy Development*: The process to formulate and update strategy.
- *Strategy Management*: Design and report on objectives and measures.
- *Organization Alignment*: Ensure alignment of all organization levels with the strategy.
- *Planning & Budgeting*: Link to strategy.
- *Human Capital Alignment*: Ensure alignment of each individual with the strategy.
- *Strategy Communications*: A comprehensive communication and education process focused on strategy.
- *Initiative Management*: Identify and oversee management of strategic initiatives.

- *Strategy Review Process*: Ensure effectiveness of strategy review and learning meetings.
- *Best Practice Sharing*: Facilitate process to identify and share best practices.

Leaders have the ultimate responsibility for strategy in an organization. It is important the whole organization is clear on what strategy is. Strategy implies going from here to there. The organization never was there before. And "there" implies new customers, new products, new attitudes, and new culture in the organization. Dr. Norton said: "Strategy is about taking an organization from where it is today and taking it to some place it has never been before; to do that you have to execute change." Strategy management tools are useful to facilitate this change. But it helps to start with a broader view of the process. It is important on how the transformation is managed to lead the organization to successfully execute its strategy. Common *weaknesses* that exist within leadership and ownership scope are described below:

- ✗ Not initiating a change program with strong, continued focus on the day-to-day activities.
- ✗ Employee engagement and support is not enough.
- ✗ Not ensuring a clear sequence of activities, based on corporate priorities, and separate change activities from business-as-usual.
- ✗ Not being consistent and methodical in approach.
- ✗ Not empowering key individuals and trusting them to lead change.
- ✗ Not nurturing future leaders and future visionaries.
- ✗ Not creating a platform to challenge and agree corporate priorities.
- ✗ Not ensuring all players has access to this platform, particularly the uncommitted.
- ✗ Fostering collaboration and cooperation among key staff is not enough.

- ✖ Not making strategy the central agenda in all reviews and meetings.
- ✖ Not appointing clear team/leader with primary responsibility for facilitating and driving strategy execution.
- ✖ Regularly communicating benefits not enough.
- ✖ Not able to anticipate change in behaviors.
- ✖ Not ensuring clear roles and responsibilities in owning initiatives.
- ✖ Not encouraging transparency.
- ✖ Unable to manage issues at appropriate levels.

Some organizations begin by creating awareness of the need for change in their organizations. Sometimes this is obvious. If the organization is losing million of dollars per day, it is obvious that change is required. In other cases, there are organizations that are leading their industry, but anticipate the impact of e-commerce, or some other global change that is taking place. So they use strategic initiative to get the organization moving. Strategy requires a vision for where the organization is going, and a plan to get there.

In short, it is the responsibility of leaders to strategically manage the organization. Strategy management is a continuous process rather than a one-time event. Therefore, leaders must become strategic thinkers of the organization and its culture, changing it as necessary. To be the most successful, leaders need to be facilitators, coaches, consultants, and consensus-builders. Transformational leadership is described by Bernard Bass as, "superior leadership performance that occurs when leaders broaden and elevate the interests of their employees, when they generate awareness and acceptance of the purposes and mission of the group, and when they stir their employees to look beyond their own self interest for the good of the group". Acquiring transformational leadership traits requires hard work and dedication, willingness to take some risks, and internalizing the organization's vision and guiding principles.

The important and critical items on the leadership and ownership check list are designed to address the content, process, and impact of leadership and ownership during strategy development and execution phase. The recommended items are described in the following *check list*:

- ✓ Powerful change management capabilities exist.
- ✓ Awareness of need to change and desire to change.
- ✓ Organizations need to commit the key people that they feel the change as a solution and not as a problem.
- ✓ Knowledge to do the change by understanding the major issues.
- ✓ Identify the players, sponsor, advocates, targets, and black-holes.
- ✓ Prepare specific change actions and detailed plans.
- ✓ Implementation of a knowledge management model.
- ✓ Leadership plays a critical role in cultural transformation.
- ✓ Role of change and transformation manager in each organization is needed.
- ✓ Relationships should be shown and communicated visually with the use of a strategy map.
- ✓ Transparency needs to be present in order for the cause & effect relationships to be revealed.
- ✓ Managers receive relevant financial and operational information in a timely manner.
- ✓ Need to increase culture of transparency and knowledge management.

CHAPTER 5

STRATEGY MANAGEMENT AUTOMATION

CHAPTER 5: STRATEGY MANAGEMENT AUTOMATION

This chapter introduces a decision framework that can assist organizations in the selecting the right strategy management software application that matches their individual organizational requirements. This chapter focuses on the following three main reasons to implement strategy management software:

- Integrates data from disparate data sources.
- Allows comprehensive data analysis.
- Facilitates organization-wide communication of the strategy.

In the present time, dashboards and strategy management applications are rapidly gaining popularity as companies invest in tools to increase the visibility, timeliness, and accuracy of Key Performance Indicators (KPIs). According to AMR Research recent survey of more than 400 organizations using strategy management products, large companies led the recent wave with 26% implementing strategy management products over the past two years and 13% currently implementing. That wave is now moving toward midsize companies, with 15% currently implementing and 34% evaluating them.[104]

Deploying a strategy is more than planning, alignment, communication, and change management. Many organizations prefer to use a software application to help pull together strategy implementation. Today, most existing software applications cannot fully manage the information contained in the strategy. This is because most systems are transaction based, such as Enterprise Resource Planning (ERP) programs. It is estimated that less than half of the information for feeding

---

104   Jacqueline Coolidge and Marc-A. Meunier, Making Enterprise Dashboards and Scorecards a Success, 2/1/2005, AMR Research, pp. 1-12

the strategy can be derived from transaction-based systems, such as ERP systems. Most of the information is stand-alone, such as customer surveys, employee suggestions, and other independent sources. Therefore, full automation of the strategy can be somewhat a challenge. However, for companies seeking to deploy the strategy through automation, there are several *advantages* including:[105]

- ✓ Provides users with rapid access to exception alerts.
- ✓ Allows easy drill down to more details about measurements and targets.
- ✓ Easy to follow dependency paths show cause and effect relationships.
- ✓ Flexibility on making changes to the strategy, including organizational changes.
- ✓ Graphical reporting of measurements and relationships.
- ✓ Facilitates control over who can see what within the strategy system.
- ✓ Wide on-line distribution of company vision and strategy.
- ✓ Analysis of strategy on-line.
- ✓ Test relations against actual data for fine-tuning the strategy.
- ✓ Integration with other desktop applications.
- ✓ Pre-defined templates and other applications make it easy to change and update different components of strategy.
- ✓ Drives rapid deployment of the strategy with minimal manual effort.

The enormous interest and embracing of strategic planning has led to the emergence of a many service businesses revolving around strategy management. Numerous consultants offer

---

105   Matt H. Evans,, Course 11: The Balanced Scorecard, 2/1/2002, Excellence in Financial Management, pp. 2-38

facilitation services to companies wishing to develop strategy. All major conference organizers offer events on the strategic planning and software vendors offer packaged applications to support strategy implementations. [106]

The use of strategy management and business intelligence (BI) applications is increasing by organizations at all levels. This chapter will discuss the case for using software applications to support strategy implementations. In addition, it will focus on one particular challenge facing many organizations; how to select the right IT infrastructure and software to support strategy implementation.

According to Andre de Waal, "one of the many performance management challenges organizations need to address is embracing information transparency in order to have the right information available at the right time, to make the best decisions, and to take actions."

Alison Classe noted that paper and pencil, or simple spreadsheet tools are everything the organization need to start applying its strategy, but if management decides to make the method an integral part of the business, automation will usually be necessary. Paul Sharman and Bruce Kavan added that paper-based measurement systems are too slow, cumbersome, labor intensive and unreliable. Also, early strategy implementations used simple Microsoft Excel-based spreadsheets to track and report strategy data, but this too, put a burden on individuals if not correctly networked and automated.

According to a KPMG study, 86% of companies use Microsoft Excel spreadsheets to support a strategy tracking as either a standalone tool or in conjunction with other tools. Major

---

106   Bernard Marr and Andy Neely, Automating the balanced scorecard – selection criteria to identify appropriate software applications, VOL. 7 2003, Measuring Business Excellence , pp. 29-36

weaknesses of standard spreadsheet documents are listed below:

- ✗ No scalability where strategy data quickly reach the capacity desktop spreadsheets can handle.
- ✗ Time-consuming to manually feed and update, which is slow and leaves enormous room for errors.
- ✗ No collaboration and communication support where data is stored in individual spreadsheets, often scattered around on different machines, and it requires big discipline to work on the same spreadsheet.
- ✗ Difficult to analyze because data is stored in individual spreadsheets, it is difficult and time consuming to bring them together for analysis.

Today, many applications exist to coordinate and manage data that relates to the strategy. Most organizations that develop and implement strategy recognize the need for effective reporting system. This reporting system makes it easy to aggregate data across strategy details. Robert Kaplan noted that strategy software helps organizations become strategy-focused by:

- ✓ Providing a visual representation of their strategy.
- ✓ Cascading high-level strategic goals down to customized objectives in business units, shared services and corporate staff units.
- ✓ Communicating performance to all employees.
- ✓ Making strategy a continual process by providing a new reporting and feedback framework.
- ✓ Technology can be integrated into the processes and culture of the organization.
- ✓ Encourage people to use technology and improve sharing of information.

In summary, the following three reasons can be considered as the main ones for managers to implement a strategy software application:

- *Data Integration*: Strategy software allows organizations to integrate data from multiple data sources (Missroon, 1998).
- *Data Analysis and Storing*: Strategy software allows organizations to analyze the data across all data sets of the scorecard, qualitative and quantitative (Silk, 1998).
- *Communication and Collaboration*: Strategy software can facilitate communication of performance data among users, top down and bottom up (McCann, 2000) and enable collaboration and feedback loops (Silk, 1998).

However, various authors draw attention to the fact that software is only a tool and not a substitute for the initial hard work of strategic analysis. Software enables organizations to implement the strategy organization-wide with one precondition, that employees will use it. Therefore it is important to pick a solution that meets the requirements of the organization in order to ensure the usage and subsequent success of strategy implementation.

Today, technology plays a unique and critical role in market place. It's a common component among the market leaders. While it can never replace gut feel and intuition, it can provide managers with early alerts and trend analysis which will help them take proactive action to ensure their goals and objectives are met, and if not, why they aren't. Technology also gives employees a view across the entire organization and the ability to work in a cross-functional and collaborative fashion, compared to the silo management style that could slow the company progress.

Strategy management applications are in use at leading organizations to manage their goals and metrics in a collaborative way. These IT products have the ability to help the organization manage its goals and objectives, take action where necessary to ensure success, and decide on future strategies, goals, and courses of action to improve the organization's performance. These IT products help organizations improve their performance, and it represents the next generation of technology to help market leaders stay ahead of the competition.[107]

Organizations need to understand, optimize, and align their business and processes to ensure they reach stated goals by leveraging information and analytics. Whether organizations choose to widely implement enterprise performance management or focus on more tactical-oriented initiatives, it is good strategy management that enables organizations to more effectively align their business strategy with execution. Common *weaknesses* in the automation process of strategy and performance management include the following list items below:[108]

- ✗ Organization does not embrace information transparency.
- ✗ Right information is not available at the right time to the right decision maker.
- ✗ Organization's employees do not use or utilize the software.
- ✗ Cost of developing strategy management software goes out of control.

---

107   Guy Weismantel, An Enterprise Approach to Performance Management, 6/26/2005, Business Objects,

108   Smith, Mark. "Business Planning or Business Performance Management?" Intelligent Enterprise, September 24, 2002.

5.1 The Software Marketplace

Today, we can easily find in excess of 30 different organizations all of whom are willing to offer strategy management and business intelligence (BI) applications. For an overview of some software vendors offering strategy management solutions, see table below. Each vendor has unique advantages for its particular product. Each vendor will be able to demonstrate applications of his product and provide credentials from satisfied users. To choose the right application, the organization has to:

- Go through the process of making the right decision to automate and get leadership support.
- Cut down the list from 30 to three or four on the shortlist to study.
- Decide which of these different few vendors to go with.

Software vendors with solutions that support strategy management are listed below in Table 4: [109]

---

109   Bernard Marr and Andy Neely, Automating the balanced scorecard – selection criteria to identify appropriate software applications, VOL. 7 2003, Measuring Business Excellence , pp. 29-36

Table 4: Strategy Management Vendors Details

Company name	Product name	Internet address
Active Strategy	Active Strategy Enterprise	www.activestrategy.com
Cognos	Metrics Manager	www.cognos.com
Comshare	MPC	www.comshare.com
Corporater	Corporater Balanced Scorecard	www.corporater.com
CorVu	CorStrategy/CorBusiness	www.corvu.com
Crystal Decision	Balanced Scorecard Analytic App.	www.crystaldecisions.com
Dialog Software	Dialog Strategy	www.dialogstrategy.com
EFM Software	BV Bizzscore	www.efmsoftware.com
Ergometrics	Ergometrics	www.ergometrics.com
Hyperion	Hyperion Performance Scorecard	www.hyperion.com
IC Community	Dolphin Navigator System	www.icvisions.com
IFS	IFS Scorecard	www.ifsworld.com
InPhase Software	Performance Plus	www.inphase.com
Insightformation	Balanced Scorecard Framework	www.insightformation.com
Nexance	NeXancePM	www.necance.com
MicroSoft	Performance Point	www.microsoft.com
Open Ratings	SPImact Balanced Scorecard	www.openratings.com
Oracle	Oracle Balanced Scorecard	www.oracle.com
Panorama Business Views	PB Views	www.pbviews.com
Peoplesoft	Enterprise Scorecard	www.peoplesoft.com
Pilot Software	Pilot Balanced Scorecard	www.pilotsoftware.com
Predicate Logic	TychoMetrics	www.tychometrics.com
Procos AG	Strat&Go Balanced Scorecard	www.procos.com
ProDacapo	Prodacapo Balanced Scorecard	www.prodacapo.com
QPR Software	QPR ScoreCard	www.qprsoftware.com
SAP	SEM Balanced Scorecard	www.sap.com
SAS Institute	Strategic Performance Mgmt.	www.sas.com
Show Business Software	Action Driven BSC	www.showbusiness.com
Stratsys	AB Run your company	www.runyourcompany.com
The Vision	Web Scorecard.nl	www.scorecard.nl
Vision Grupo	Consultorues Strategos	www.visiongc.com
4GHI Solutions	Cockpit Communicator	www.4ghi.com

During 2007, over $15 billion strategy management and business intelligence (BI) applications mergers and acquisitions were announced. These acquisitions are causing the debate on the most fundamental issue in enterprise software today; whether it is better for companies to have their software supplied by a few mega vendors or by a range of independent vendors.

During the past 15 years, the market has been well served by many vendors offering open systems solutions, designed to operate with a variety of databases, operating systems, web servers, application servers, and portal technologies. Many different platform vendors have been part of this market at one time or another, each delivering innovative ideas and solutions to meet the rapidly evolving business requirements for strategy management and BI platforms.

With the completion of the announced acquisitions, seven significant vendors remained: MicroStrategy, IBI, IBM, Microsoft, Oracle, SAP, and SAS. Only three of these vendors (MicroStrategy, SAS, and IBI) will continue to be independent and optimized for open systems solutions. The remaining providers, as part of multinational software companies, will operate in the more protected, closed environments of their parent companies.[110]

Many big companies genuinely prefer to purchase all of their software from single source multinational vendors. There are companies who see themselves as IBM shops, Oracle shops, Microsoft shops, or SAP shops. These companies prefer the default decision-making inherent in buying into a closed system solution. On the vendor side, Business Objects, Cognos, and Hyperion will enjoy a new and easy lock-in with these types of customers that they never enjoyed before as independent vendors.

Another significant issue for most organizations is cost. Typically the cost of developing strategy management software can cost in the region of $100,000, for even a simple application. The reporting software package prices vary enormously from a few thousand dollars to far over a million dollars, with typical spends and investments in the region of $200,000 for reasonable sized organizations. Here it is important to check not just license

---

110   MicroStrategy Incorporated, Bi Market Consolidation: Re-Igniting The Debate Of
        Open Systems Vs. Closed Systems, 1/1/2007, MicroStrategy Incorporated, pp. 2-8

fees but also maintenance fees, which can fluctuate between 10 and 25 percent of the license fees. Software pricing is a very difficult issue and different pricing models might be more applicable to a certain organization than others (i.e. pricing per user versus pricing per package). However, software companies are often flexible in their pricing and pricing models are subject to negotiation. It is also important to consider training and implementation costs as they can drastically increase the overall price of solutions, but often remain initially hidden.

Making the wrong decision by buying the wrong software, can not only result in a significant waste of time, energy and money, but can also undermine the entire strategy development and execution effort and the credibility of the performance management system. This decision process is a fundamental one and needs to be taken with great care.

There is a wide range of applications for strategy management, the potential user base is diverse, and the data access requirements are often complex. The field of vendors to consider comprises the following groups:

- *Business Intelligence (BI) Tools*: These tools are designed to enable end users the highest level of interactivity with information. They do not provide business content, and are best suited for companies that want to build their own dashboards and scorecards based on their own set of KPIs and reports, and have the appropriate resources to do so.
- *Analytics Applications*: These applications provide a good degree of standard business content, and generally provide a sufficient toolset to customize dashboards and scorecards and aggregate data from multiple sources.
- *Enterprise Applications*: Dashboards and scorecards from Enterprise Resource Planning (ERP) and other

enterprise application vendors tend to provide the highest degree of business context and the closest integration to their transactional systems. However, the ease of implementation and the off-the-shelf business content can be offset by limited customization and external data integration capabilities.

- *Infrastructure*: Enterprise Application Integration (EAI), Business Activity Monitoring (BAM), and portal vendors deliver a platform for deploying dashboards and scorecards that leverage their real-time data and support complex integration requirements. They generally provide limited business content and support for interactive analysis and drill-down.[111]

Organizations interested in strategy management application can meet the necessary information requirements of all the company constituencies. The system must be able to drive organizational alignment, visibility, and collaboration across the extended enterprise. Empowered business users need an intuitive, personalized view that delivers powerful, interactive insight.

Once management and IT have effectively deployed strategy management application, they will find objectives easier to monitor, manage, and improve. This, in turn, will allow the organization to strive towards even higher performance goals. As Intelligent Enterprise states, "Strategy management becomes an upward spiral that enables a corporation to set higher performance goals that can be attained realistically, predictably, and confidently."[112]

111   Jacqueline Coolidge and Marc-A. Meunier, Making Enterprise Dashboards and Scorecards a Success, 2/1/2005, AMR Research, pp. 1-12
112   Russom, Philip. "Five Easy Pieces." Intelligent Enterprise, October 8, 2002. Copyright CMP Media LLC.

5.2 Evaluation Criteria and Selection

In order to develop a good selection framework the organization management has to realize that there are numerous members of organizations influencing the selection process with very different agendas. It is common to see that IT directors looked at the IT infrastructure and integration capabilities; finance directors looked for the economically most sensible solutions; business analysts looked for the most comprehensive analysis capabilities; and general managers looked for a good user interface and ease of use. This meant that the evaluation criteria and selection has to consider multiple views from multiple members in the organization.

In turn, to select an appropriate strategy support system, the organization could create a project plan with an established timeline for selecting and implementing the software. Typical timeframes span from a few weeks to months, depending on system integration and the number of stockholder involved. The project plan should include the following steps:

- Develop a short list: research vendor options based on general pricing, on commitment to strategy software, and on the vendor's financial health.
- Submit a request for proposal (RFP) with the following components:
  - List functional requirements (i.e. display options, interfaces, and analysis capabilities).
  - Technical requirements (i.e. operating platform, database compatibility).
  - Operational requirements (i.e. technology and user license fees, training, support).
- Arrange product demonstrations: use the same evaluation rating criteria, ask to demonstrate specific tasks, and develop standard questions for each vendor.
- Create a summary report and select software.

It is important to recognize that each organization has a unique set of requirements for a strategy management software application and it is not possible to provide a single list of requirements appropriate for every organization. Organizations differ in terms of size, IT infrastructure, communication style, required level of security, cash position, scorecard design, IT literacy, and in-house capabilities. All these aspects affect the selection criteria of a strategy management software solution. This research presents a set of criteria that organizations could consider. Later, they could assign weight for each one to reflect their unique set of requirements.

Following the same logic, the 30 or so different strategy management packages that are available on the market each have different strengths and weaknesses. Particular packages will be relevant for one organization for particular reasons, while they may be completely inappropriate for another. So rather than worrying only about the packages on the market, the organization should think first about what its needs are from strategy management application. The easiest way is to create a two-directional matrix in which organizations put weightings against each criteria, this matrix can then be used to compare available software product against the organizational. When comparing software options, the organization could keep in mind that it's not the quantity of information that matters (quantity is never lacking); it's the quality. Common *weaknesses* in the evaluation and selection of strategy and performance management software include the following issues listed below: [113]

- ✗ Mismatch among strategy management software and IT infrastructure.
- ✗ Organization needs and business requirements are not met.

---

113   Travis Manzione,, Driving the new management meeting with technology, 4/1/2006, Balanced Scorecard Report, pp. 15-16

- ✘ Making the wrong decision by involving wrong team-members.
- ✘ Evaluation criteria is bias, not balanced, or based on hidden agenda.

In the following section defines the selection criteria that companies could discuss when evaluating strategy management software:

- The Product
  - ○ Product presence in the region (customer base)
  - ○ Product overall reputation in market
  - ○ Market feedback on product
  - ○ Product ability to meet multi-unit business needs
  - ○ Total cost (initial & license fees)
  - ○ Ability to deliver as planned
  - ○ Information on past similar implementation
  - ○ Software design reflecting the functions and operations of the system
  - ○ Link solution designs to the Functional and Non Functional Requirements
  - ○ Demonstrates capability being designed against stakeholders' requirements
  - ○ Traceability Matrix Requirements
  - ○ Systems Requirements Specifications (SRS) document
  - ○ Security layer design

- Data Sources
  - ○ Integration with appropriate data sources
  - ○ Ability to gather the necessary data for transformation
  - ○ Accommodate scalability for large data sets
  - ○ Extensibility for adding more data
  - ○ Import / export data

- Integration & Transformation
  - ° Automate data integration from disparate data sources
  - ° Design integration platforms and data transformation requirements
  - ° Connectors to identified systems
  - ° Enterprise Service Bus that connects data to the warehouse
  - ° ETL (Extract Transfer Load) module to cater to existing data formats
  - ° System Architecture that explicitly cover all components blocks
  - ° System Architecture that comply with Standards

- Data Warehouse
  - ° Archiving functionality
  - ° Ability to easily load data into data warehouse
  - ° Employ appropriate model for unstructured data
  - ° Business continuity (provide continual access)
  - ° Design data sources block
  - ° Design Disaster Recovery Plan
  - ° Alarm features (trigger e-mail for responsible person)
  - ° Data update traceability (audit trails)
  - ° Easy to do data entry (populate data warehouse)

- Analytics
  - ° Optimize for rapid analysis
  - ° Support online queries through remote access systems (e.g. OLAP)
  - ° Data mining & explanatory features
  - ° Data modeling & trend analysis (i.e. historical data)
  - ° Data forecasting & simulation
  - ° Ability to add comments next to actual data and gaps (all levels)
  - ° Exception alerting notifications (i.e. out of range, empty)

- ° Reporting & Presentation
- ° Design presentation and reporting solutions based on users needs
- ° Support multi-languages
- ° Design User Interface Requirements
- ° Report archiving & lifecycle
- ° Provide reports remotely
- ° Ad-hoc reporting
- ° Strategy maps or cause & effect type diagrams
- ° Various charts types
- ° Data mapping & trends
- ° Traffic lights identified and generated to all levels
- ° Drilling-down and up can be performed within the system
- ° Scorecard, dashboard, & Business Intelligence
- ° Ability of end-user to create own reports (with ease and speed)
- ° Workflow (i.e. approval)
- ° Design the decision support capabilities
- ° Web-enabled reports
- ° Multiple views / dimensions to see same data
- ° Define graphical user interface (GUI)

- • Support & Maintenance
  - ° Provision of online help necessary to support operation of the system
  - ° Ensure a high level of response to software issues and upgrades
  - ° Provision of a capability for system enhancements
  - ° Company track record in maintaining product support after delivery

5.3 Scalability and Flexibility

First, it is a good idea to check basic product information. In terms of company, it might be good to understand the background of the company and the product. Very large software companies might have only a few people working on their strategy management application, which might be treated as a byproduct. On the other hand, a small company, which specializes in performance measurement software, might have more expertise and a larger client list. The size and global presence of a software vendor might be important if organizations plan to implement the strategy management globally or across countries.

In order to assess the scalability needs, it is important to consider the final implementation scope. Companies might initially implement the strategy management in one department or business unit only, but later roll it out organization-wide. There are three aspects of scalability:

- The application should be scalable in terms of programming. It should be easy to add new scorecards at any time.
- The underlying database should be scalable as the amount of data accumulates quickly.
- The communication approach should be scalable so that it is easy to disseminate the information through the web.

Today, organizations are less willing to invest in applications that are not able to integrate with other applications. Many tools provide interfaces with reporting packages, activity-bases costing solutions, CRM or planning tools. Flexibility should also be provided in terms of methodology support. Furthermore, companies might call their approach strategy management but have altered the approach to fit its needs. For example, software should allow for such flexibility so users can create personal views or personal scorecards.

Organizations can discuss needs in terms of administrative tasks and access control, exception alerting, collaboration and reporting. It should be possible to assign owners and people responsible for data entry in order to contact them or even send them automated reminders. Some organizations like automated workflows, other organizations do not feel that such an approach fits their work culture. Organizations might want the software to support action and include activity or project fields that allow tracking progress against strategic objectives. Organizations need to decide about the level of security needed in the system; some companies are very open and share any aspect of strategy management among all employees whereas others require tight security. Language can also be an issue for international organizations and they might want to check whether the application support various languages at once.

The technical requirements depend on the existing infrastructure in each organization. Any new piece of software should support the existing desktop or network operating system. It is important for strategy management application to extract data from existing data sources, which can be a major obstacle for any implementation. The strategy management usually requires information from a variety of different databases as well as text based data. It is also worth to check the browser compatibility as few software tools only support MS Internet Explorer. The IT department should be involved in the discussion about technical requirements.

Vendors offer different levels of service. Some offer no implementation support and instead partner with consulting companies. Other vendors offer comprehensive service including own implementation service and international service hotline. Organizations need to be clear how much support they want and whether the vendor or its partners can deliver this.

Common *weaknesses* in the scalability and flexibility of strategy and performance management software include the issues listed below:

- ✗ Software scalability is limited and does not address organization on-going needs.
- ✗ The chosen software can't integrate with other applications or data sources.
- ✗ Software is not flexible enough in terms of organization methodology support.
- ✗ Security of information becomes an issue after the implementation of software.
- ✗ Vendor software support is weak or decrease over time.

5.4 Business Intelligence and Dashboards

Organizations have to decide how they want the data to be presented. Applications vary between very graphical to more text and tables based. One of the most important aspects is the display of strategy maps. If organizations use this powerful way to visualize the cause-and-effect relationships it is important that the software packages support those dynamically. Some tools just display graphics without any real dynamic views. Dynamic maps allow organizations to use it as the main communication tool with traffic lighting.

Numerous data points and the ability to manage measures and manipulate data are critical to the line manager for operational performance review, but the senior manager or executive conducting a strategic performance review needs only a top-level view of performance against objectives and initiatives. So, the software should be capable of presenting data and analysis at the big-picture, organizational level, which is critical to making strategic decisions, while offering drilldown capability for each successive level below.[114]

Improving corporate performance requires visibility horizontally across organizational groups and vertically within business units. This means that after the company has been aligned through commonly defined objectives, teams can track and analyze the defined metrics that exist primarily in their domain as well as those relevant KPIs that span over multiple groups. With the ability to have real-time visibility into their own departmental processes and to experience how those processes connect with those of other groups, dashboard empowered organizations can become far more responsive and effective in a changing environment.

---

114   Travis Manzione, Driving the new management meeting with technology, 4/1/2006, Balanced Scorecard Report, pp. 15-16

Tools offer different levels of analysis capabilities, stretching from simple drill-down capabilities to multi-dimensional analysis, complex statistical functionality, forecasting and even scenario planning. Companies that require more complex analysis functionality often have tools for this in place and have to decide whether to integrate or replace them. Analysis functionality also includes the number of graphical displays form bar charts to advanced 3-D charts and tolerance settings. Requirements in terms of charts and graphs depend on the measures the organization tracks and their visualization requirements. For this discussion, it is especially important to include the business analysis. In addition, any technology solution the organization considers should enable drilldown reporting. The ability to view and analyze cascaded relationships and their impact on enterprise wide outcomes is critical.

Whether management chooses to implement strategy management application or focus on specific departments and processes, management dashboards have become the foundation of most performance-driven management initiatives. These web-based dashboards provide business users with an intuitive graphical console of metrics, or key performance indicators (KPIs), for monitoring and analyzing progress towards defined organizational goals. With the right combination of dashboard technology, performance indicators, and business methodologies, organizations are working towards better aligning their business strategy with execution.[115]

Collaboration features are important when organizations share complex decision making across various parties to reach shared group goals. This is a necessary capability because many business problems do not occur in isolation and are not solvable by one person. Often, more heads are better than one. Complex problems can benefit from joint decision making, where the

---

115   Jason Kuo, Management Dashboards Enabling Performance Management
       across the Enterprise, 10/1/2002, Business Objects

analysis and intellectual insight of numerous people or groups result in a more balanced response or optimal solution.

Collaboration also includes sharing objectives and decision making with customers and suppliers via an extranet dashboard. These partners may not be in the organization, but are crucial to many of the organization's processes. Today, extranet dashboards have already gained popularity and are being deployed widely to improve customer relations, align supply chains, and link partners to the overall business.

Gartner has noted that the trend towards using extranet dashboards between organizations for more collaboration must involve the joint definition of metrics, which reinforces win-win relationships. For instance, many organizations are sharing service line agreement and other performance-related metrics with their customers via dashboard extranets. Metrics show aggregated compliancy while case specifics are available by drilling down from the metric to more detailed reports. Alerts warn all parties of possible obstacles so that issues can be fixed before critical milestones are completed. Common *weaknesses* in using Business Intelligence and dashboards for strategy and performance management software include the issues listed below:

- ✗ Cause-and-effect relationships that the software packages support are not dynamic enough.
- ✗ Business Intelligence design is poor and not communicating information to end-user in a clear manner.
- ✗ Analysis capabilities are weak and data can not be studied and analyzed.
- ✗ Collaboration features are not there where decision making across various parties is not supported within the application.

❄ ❄ ❄

5.5 Reporting and Data Presentation

The communication aspect of any strategy implementation is a key. Organizations have to address issues such as; web-enabled software; users able to comment on strategy, objectives, measures, activities; and security restrictions. Some software solutions are able to trigger automatic alerts, e-mails or SMS messages, which can be sent to individuals or groups indicating that certain areas of the business are under performing and action is required. For most implementations it is important that the strategy management software supports e-mail and comments. In turn, they could be attached or linked to performance reviews or analysis results.

It should also provide a report printing capability to enable offline reporting and review. Reporting is a chief input to any strategic knowledge management mechanism. Many organizations choose to automate this function in order to share strategy information widely throughout the organization.

The strategy management report should include an overview of each area's strategy map, list of action items from financial results, objectives and measures, and initiative updates. The report should be able to generate an appendix that includes definitions of measures and initiatives, as well as any other important documents, such as list of the individuals accountable for each performance area. Effective reporting software allows data and analysis to be assembled in a brief report that supports leaders' ability to make timely and sound decisions. With the right reporting tool, reports will serve as the springboard for effective management meetings and help to keep the focus directly on strategy execution.[116]

---

116 Travis Manzione,, Driving the new management meeting with technology, 4/1/2006, Balanced Scorecard Report, pp. 15-16

When the organization allows greater access to performance information, people can easily learn whether strategy is working, and which units, departments, and teams are doing a better job. A defined and structured knowledge management system makes it possible to document the reasons for high performance, to disseminate this information broadly throughout the organization, and to educate and train others about how they can improve their performance.

One of the goals of strategy management software is often to reform the reporting culture of the organization. The objective of this reform is to move from a practice where every single piece of information is reported just in case the data is needed to more dynamic information sharing where everyone can access exactly the information they need. Strategy management software provides a big amount of dynamical views into the information contained in the system. All views can be used as reports as such and distributed also on paper if needed. In addition to the ready made dynamical views of the data, organization can also create customized reports by integrating its existing reporting system with the software. Most reports can be published through the system Portal. This way the users can access all management information through the same easy-to-use interface. Common *weaknesses* in reporting and data presentation of strategy and performance management software include the issues listed below:[117]

- ✗ The software package is not web-enabled software.
- ✗ Report capability of the software is weak and reports are not easy to be generated and printed.
- ✗ Visibility is not clear horizontally across organizational groups and vertically within business units.
- ✗ The software does not support structured knowledge management system.

117   Balanced Scorecard Collaborative, QPR ScoreCard, 1/1/2004, QPR Software Plc

CHAPTER 6

CONCLUSION

CHAPTER 6 CONCLUSION

This chapter summarizes the main points discussed in past chapters. The conclusion of this book indicates that weaknesses exist throughout strategic plan development and execution processes. The main weaknesses discussed in this chapter are; over-engineered or weak strategic plan; increasingly complex environment; weak leadership skills; strategic plan weak link to budget; usage of confusing and inconsistent terminology; unreasonable time period from planning to execution; lack of education and training of staff; lack of executive commitment; forced cascading approach; absence of IT strategy management tool; and finally management driven by short-term wins.

6.1 Summary of Main Issues

Writing this book was an attempt to provide a context for understanding the critical factors that lead to successful implementation of strategic plans. According to Fortune Magazine, less than ten percent of strategies effectively formulated are effectively executed. This book aims at exploring strategic planning and the implementation process to clarify why very few organizations effectively implement their strategic plan while so many other organizations fail to do so. In addition, part of this book is dedicated to identifying the most effective tools and methods to successfully implement a strategic plan.

A positive and strong relationship exists between the development of a strategic plan and its successful execution later on. This conclusion supports strategy thinkers like Chester Barnard (The Functions of The Executive, 1938), Alfred Chandler (Strategy and Structure, 1962), and Ken Andrews (The Concept of Corporate Strategy, 1971) who emphasized the strong relationship between developing and implementing strategy. There is a clear and unambiguous relationship between defining goals, objectives, measures and initiatives and their execution. In addition, one of the problems for strategy execution is over-engineered strategic plans which are difficult to understand and involve too many variables.

Developing and executing strategy increasingly becoming a complex process, particularly taking internal and external scanning factors into account. On one hand, critics of the environmental scanning process state that all scanning does, is spending a great deal of time collecting data that is mostly irrelevant or already known. On the other hand, Dr. Stoffels' viewpoint emphasizes on environmental scanning as a methodology that may be difficult to observe or diagnose but that cannot be ignored. In addition, many researches' results indicated that the problems for strategy execution is not doing enough testing and understanding of the surrounding environment.[118]

Increased complexity in more challenging internal and external environments requires stronger framework for execution across the organization, which many organizations today do not have. Without managing strategy and performance in a consistent and adaptable way to the environment, the organization would not reach stated targets and the complexity of executing the strategy would be too overwhelming for the whole organization. Therefore, successfully implementation of strategy requires an integrated way of management for many interrelated disciplines, approaches, and processes.

Leadership skills are becoming more important in increasingly complex environment. Leaders can effect change more readily by driving the timetable for strategy execution and demonstrating sustained commitment by leading from the front. Leading from the front entails not to download this responsibility to "strategy team" or "consultants" but instead showing personal commitment to change; winning hearts and minds through good facilitation and influencing; making strategy relevant to the individual; and linking leader's personal objectives to successful execution of the strategy. All being done while continually monitoring the corporate climate and maintaining high levels of motivation and a positive outlook. In addition, leadership is especially important in being able to take calculated risks. This means being able to take bold decisions while having developed an acute sense of awareness of the internal and external environments.

It seems important to monitor the characteristics of the top leadership team who is responsible to develop and implement the organization strategic plan. Dr. Robert Kaplan emphasized

---

118   Stoffels, J. Strategic Issues Management: A Comprehensive Guide to Environmental Scanning, Pergamon, 1994, pp. 1.

on creating "Office of Strategy Management" in the organization. Dr. Kaplan mentioned that bringing qualified people to help guide the organization in strategic issues is a good step forward. Currently this is not emphasized enough on leadership skills of top management. Leadership appears to be a consistent weakness in the organizations and could be one of the main reasons why strategy execution is not happening in a smooth and strong manner.

With regards to linking strategic planning to management *budget processes*, Gary Hamel and C. K. Prahalad [119] stated that most organizations rely on the budget process to bridge the gap between long-term strategic plans and detailed short-term annual plans. Many critics tend to disagree with this conclusion because budget like any other resource could be forecasted based on a long-term strategic plan. Short term budget is needed to give managers the right financing to execute the initiatives on the strategic plans for one year. Dr. David Norton rightly identified financial budget as a controlled way to allocate financial resources that can be tracked and utilized with reasonable effectiveness. Financial budget is not a strong tool to promote a long-term view. It was not meant for communicating strategy or for target setting. In short, financial budget is a necessary tool for managing the allocation of financial resources. To manage strategy and operations, the organization must use other systems. Dr. Norton added that embedding the strategic planning into management processes such as budgeting allows organizations to tap the full potential of a dynamic framework. However, premature attempts to establish these links may cause a rapid decline in strategy momentum. [120]

Terminology surfaced as a concern for people working for government or large corporations. The usage of confusing

---

119   Gary Hamel and C.K. Prahalad, Competing for the Future, Harvard Business
       School Press, 1994, pp. 120-121
120   David P. Norton, Philip W. Peck,, Linking Operations to Strategy and Budgeting,
       10/1/2008, Balanced Scorecard Report, pp. 1-6

terminology in the strategic plans and performance management tends to be a common issue. It is common to see participants request to simplify the strategic planning and performance management process by using clearer and more consistent terminology. For example, key performance indicators are not like objectives yet many organizations use the two terms to describe the same thing. Everyone needs to be speaking the same language if measurement is to be used in guiding change within an organization. It is the responsibility of management to publish approved terminology or glossary of terms for all managers, staff, and consultants to use. It is common to see strategic review meetings when it suddenly becomes obvious that not everyone in the room is on the same page. Translating strategy into execution is hard enough, but when not all managers can even agree on the same language, the situation can become even more challenging.

With regards to time it takes to develop and implement a strategy, the act of translating strategy into measurable objectives does force specificity. Forcing specificity does help to surface and resolve those hidden disagreements that often get buried when the strategy remains vague, only to return at some later date to haunt an organization.[121] But on the other hand, the issue of using strategy management to solve all hidden disagreements might extend the time it takes to develop and implement the organization strategy.

The task of having clear, unambiguous relationships between goals, objectives, measures and initiatives is important but the time and effort required to establish these relationships can become a concern by itself. To some organizations, the nature of its work makes the definition of the relationships among strategic plan components more complicated and thus harder to define clearly. Timing tends to be an important factor

---

121   John H. Lingle, From BSC to IS Measurement, 1/1/2007, Wm. Schiemann & Associates Inc, pp. 1-6

for a successful strategy implementation in an increasingly competitive environment.

Both ends of the *time spectrum* may be sources of implementation issues, too long and too short time to implement. Some organizations will not unveil their new strategy until every measure has been developed, data sources confirmed, and clear relationship to other measures and objectives is clearly set. This factor could delay the implementation for a long time.

In contrast, there are those organizations at the opposite end of the spectrum that attempt to have a complete set of measures and objectives up and running in unreasonably short period of time. Often organizations attempt to compress the timeframe when using consultants. They feel the experience and methodologies offered by their hired experts should ensure a completed product very fast. However, developing a complete strategy with requisite cause and effect linkages weaving together unrelated measures cannot be completed overnight, nor should it be.

The need of reaching consensus on developing good objectives, measures, and targets is important. Nevertheless, the time from strategy development to implementation should be reasonable and should take into consideration lost opportunities due to slow reaction to external environment.

With regards to *education and training*, Balanced Scorecard Collaborative rightly stated that organizations that fail to educate and engage their people in strategy execution usually fail to achieve their full potential. Organizational success requires that employees are truly trained, engaged, and committed to their work and share the values and goals of the organization.[122] Lack of education and training of staff is a weakness that needs to be addressed. Past researches indicated the need to promote

---

122   Balanced Scorecard Collaborative, QPR ScoreCard, 1/1/2004, QPR Software Plc

achievements or desired strategy implementation through awareness and education. In their rush of implementing a strategy, many organizations give up upfront the effort of providing meaningful and detailed training to those expected to implement the strategy. Usually, quick awareness sessions are held during which the strategy implementation methodology is introduced on the surface, however little education is offered regarding the complexities and details of the used methodology.

In addition, it's often the deceptive simplicity of the used framework that makes people very vulnerable to the false impression that in-depth training is not required. Strategy execution framework can be simply mastered with sponsoring in-depth training and then trust employees' business instincts to kick in and fuel the development of a powerful new performance system. The cost of the decision of not providing enough training will manifest itself in a poorly executed strategy. Organizations need to take the necessary time at the beginning of the project to develop a comprehensive strategy execution training that includes background on the concept, objectives in implementing strategy, typical problems, and success stories.

Another serious challenge for strategy implementation is senior management not buying into the process. Without *executive commitment and sponsorship*, the effort of successfully implement the organization strategy is most likely to fail. Executive commitment and sponsorship is the common thread that connects the entire planning and execution process. Without a strong and vocal leader present at each stage the effort can quickly stall. Today, there is growing need for energetic and knowledgeable executives willing to work tirelessly towards the cause of advancing strategy to an efficient and effective execution.

Henry Mintzberg tried to explain why leader commitment is absent sometimes in securing strong planning and execution process. Mr. Mintzberg's argument is that leaders take advantage of strategic planning and use it as a communication tool to influence outsiders. This is when planning becomes a public relations game. Langley found this to be true of the public sector in general, where public relation becomes common motivation for strategic planning, although the same kind of role is played by subsidiaries and divisions who have to produce strategic plans for their parent firms. [123]

This view of *planning as a front wall* to impress outsiders is supported by other experts. Nutt cited that city governments sometimes hire consultants to do strategic planning to impress bond rating agencies. Cohen and March described strategic plans as symbol for a failing organization that announces a plan to succeed. They also discussed plans that become advertisements, noting that "what is frequently called a 'plan' could be really an investment brochure". Michael Porter was concerned about this issue "Strategy had lost its intellectual currency. It was losing adherents. People were being tricked and misled by other ideas," he said [124]

However, the above views are somewhat unfair and label executives as unethical and selfish. Even though commitment is an issue, the reason why this commitment is not there is way broader than a public relations game that is being played. Many executives think that strategic planning is time-consuming and long process which in most cases does not pay off. Motivation plays an important role in pushing executive commitment higher. Statistics indicates that most organizations have a problem executing their strategy. According to Fortune Magazine "Less than 10% of strategies effectively formulated are effectively executed."[125] Taking this depressing statistics into

---

123   Henry Mintzberg, The Pitfalls Of Strategic Planning, Fall, 1993, California Management Review, pp. 1-12

124   Keith Hammonds, You've got to make time for strategy, 3/1/2001, Illustrations, pp. 1-6

125   Dr. Robert Kaplan, BSC Form – Dubai, Middle East 2008

consideration, executives today could be under tremendous pressure to perform while trying to keep themselves and the people around them motivated.

In relation to *vertical alignment* used by an organization toward executing its strategy, there is a common weakness in cascading approach often used by many managers. The majority of authors and strategy experts tend to agree that it is only by cascading the strategy to all levels of the organization that a successful implementation can occur. In other words, one of the most important implementation essential for a successful strategy is the enrollment of the entire organization in its achievement. Most of the time the cascading is done by using a "forced" top to bottom approach. Front-line employees not only are usually removed from organizational high level strategy, but they are often "told by their manager" how they will contribute to their department's goal and in turn to the whole organization's goals.

Best methodology is a "combination" of both, top-down approach and bottom-up approach. First, the organization cascades down its strategy to the department or section level by using top-down approach. Secondly, employees link to their department or section goals by using bottom-up approach. This combined approach allows every employee to describe how they contribute to the organization's strategy. Soichiro Honda, founder of the Honda Motor Company, supported this recommended view on cascading strategy. He stated once that one of the most important obligations of senior leadership is to communicate what the company will be in the future, and to set goals that staff "can align to".

With regards to the use of *IT systems* to help develop, host, and execute the organization's strategy, it is not widely adopted yet. According to a KPMG study, 86% of companies use Microsoft

Excel spreadsheets to support a strategy tracking as either a standalone tool or in conjunction with other tools. If anything, this statistic is a good indication that management in general still has a long way to go on taking the decision to automate strategy. If an organization decides to make the strategy management an integral part of the business, automation will usually be necessary.

Paul Sharman and Bruce Kavan stated that paper-based measurement systems are too slow, cumbersome, labor intensive and unreliable. The decision to automate strategy management could be influenced by the financial and operational situation of the organization. For instance, purchasing a system has a big implication on the business in terms of continuous maintenance of the system (technically and functionally) and training new staff on how to use it. In addition, finding the right staff who knows how to support and maintain this system is another challenge by itself.

In relation to the use of strategic planning in the *public sector*, it didn't mature enough yet if compared with the private sector. Strategy and performance systems in public sector that people looked at as "benchmark" from the outside are mostly fragile and not stable from inside. It is true that there were many attempts by many governments to push forward the good use of strategic planning and performance management. For instance, the UK government has developed an approach that recognizes the value of local decisions about local government performance.[126] The "New Managerialism" movement of the 1980s and 1990s has seen the introduction of many government policies that supported performance management systems. Osborne and Gaebler, in their book "Reinventing Government" outlined a number of key incentives for performance management in

---

126   Robert Mellor, Performance Measurement & Management In Asian-Pacific
        Local Government, 9/1/2003, The Network of Local Government Training and
        Research, pp. 2-69

"new" public sector organizations. [127] In addition, many of the so called "Public Sector Reform" developments across the world have also introduced regimes that have a clear element of performance management. The true question should be "how effective all these attempts and regimes were?" Without knowing the results it becomes hard to conclude that public sector have been "Re-invented".

In this context, continuous and drastic changes under so called "new and better public programs" have been happening without explaining for instance, why the "old programs" failed to do the job. The mechanism of democracy could be partially the cause of this unstable evolvement of strategy implementation in public sector. For example, it is common to see that as soon as a new government takes control of managing public needs, it starts with a new way of measuring performance to guaranty that it will survive in power for the next election. Based on this behavior, most governments today are driven by short-term wins, which in many cases goes against long-term views of strategic planning, for instance, to secure better quality life for citizens.

Public sector managers need to acquire more knowledge which they need to better execute their organization strategic plan. In turn, this could improve overall effectiveness and efficiency of the government. Public sector managers have indicated their perception of good performance. Determining the extent to which governments actually tangibly provide solutions to strategy-related common weaknesses would better enable public sector managers to appropriately adjust their activities and behaviors to improve the execution quality of their organization's strategic plans. Wider communication together with focused training for middle and senior managers on how to apply the principles of strategy execution could prove very beneficial to any government. In addition, increased awareness

---

127   Osborne, D. & Gaebler, R., Reinventing Government, 1992

of public sector staff concerning the impact of their work and attitude toward the organization's strategy could play very important factor for successful execution of the strategy.

GLOSSARY

❄ ❄ ❄

V. GLOSSARY

- **Activity Based Costing**: is a cost measurement system that provides a cost for each product, service or customer by analyzing each activity needed to produce a product or service to customer.
- **Balanced Scorecards**: A system of linked objectives, measures, targets and initiatives which collectively describe the strategy of an organization and how that strategy can be achieved.
- **Balanced**: refers to the fact that companies must take a balanced approach to managing their business. All too often, businesses focus on financial measures.
- **Bayesian Inference**: A numerical estimate of the degree of belief in a hypothesis before and after the evidence has been observed.
- **Benchmarking:** The process of assessing an agency's performance in producing a service against a comparable service external to the agency.
- **Beyond Budgeting Model:** budget method designed to overcome traditional barriers and to create a flexible, adaptable organization that gives local managers self-confidence and freedom to make decisions rapidly.
- **Constraint Analysis:** The use of one or more constraint satisfaction algorithms to specify the set of feasible solutions.
- **Customer Life Cycle Management**: Measurement of customer relationship business performance over time; customer satisfaction, increase growth, enhance loyalty, decrease defections, optimize lifetime value, all the while reducing costs to serve.
- **Customer Value Management**: Method of delivery optimal value to customers by aligning business

metrics, capabilities, processes, organizational structure, infrastructure with customer-defined value.

- **Dashboard**: A related group of interactive scorecard and report views that are organized together in a single site. Dashboard elements may share common filters that control the data displayed within the elements

- **Driver-Based Causal Model**: is budget method constructed from key operational activity drivers that allow linking strategic, operational, and capital resources to the operating plan.

- **Economic Value Added**: is to monitor the overall value creation in a business. It is a method to measure the results.

- **Effectiveness indicator**: Provides information on the extent of, or progress in a reporting period towards, achievement desired outcome through the delivery of agreed services.

- **Efficiency indicator:** Relates a service to the level of resource input required to deliver it.

- **EFQM Model**: The European Foundation for Quality Management (EFQM) was originally developed as a quality award framework but its further use as an organizational improvement tool.

- **Experience Co-Creation**: Management approach that highlights the value created at the point of interaction between companies and customers; enabled by technology interface devices.

- **Future-Value Analysis**: The decomposition of market capitalization into current value and future value or expectations of future growth.

- **Goal:** An overall achievement that is considered critical to the future success of the organization. Goals express where the organization wants to be.

- **Government goal:** An expression of high level policies or priorities that support the government's vision.

Government desired outcomes contribute to these goals.

- **Indicators**: A graphical status symbol that represents where the value of a key performance indicator (KPI) is in relation to the target value. Indicators are represented by using status images and colors (indicator band colors).
- **Inputs:** The resources expended in the process of delivering services.
- **Key performance indicator**: Provides an overview of the critical or material aspects of results achievement. KPI can provide a logical and comprehensive way of describing organizational strategy behavior.
- **Lean Manufacturing**: Process management and tool set focused on the identification and reductions of 'wastes' in order to improve overall customer value, as well as to reduce production time and costs.
- **Measurement:** A way of monitoring and tracking the progress of strategic objectives. Measurements can be leading indicators of performance (leads to an end result) or lagging indicators (the end results).
- **Mission:** Broad description of what the organization does, with/for whom the organization does it, the organization distinctive competence, and why the organization does it.
- **Monte Carlo Simulation**: A computerized technique used to asses the probability of certain outcomes or risks by mathematically modeling a hypothesis event over multiple trials and comparing the outcome with predefined probability distributions.
- **Multiple Regression Analysis**: A statistical technique whereby the influence of a set of independent variables on a single dependent variable is determined.
- **Objective:** Things that specifically must be done to execute the strategy. This is doing what is critical to

the future success of the strategy. In short, what the organization must do to reach its goals.

- **Open Innovation**: Use of purposive inflows and outflows of knowledge, establish 'creation nets' to accelerate innovation and to expand the markets for external use of innovation.
- **Outcome Based Management:** It identifies the outcomes desired by top managers that agencies are expected to contribute to, and the services to be delivered to help achieve the desired outcomes. Usually, government agencies are required to identify and report outcomes and key outputs.
- **Outcome:** The effect, impact, result on, or consequence for the community, environment or target clients of government services. The reason why services are delivered.
- **Output:** A service that is standardized, so that it readily lends itself to meaningful per unit measurement.
- **Performance Target:** The current estimate of the future result to be achieved if the resources provided for that purpose are used as per the agreed plan.
- **Perspectives:** Four different views of what drives the organization. Perspectives provide a framework for measurement. The four most common perspectives are: Financial, Customer, Internal Processes, and Learning & Growth.
- **PESTEL analysis**: is a macro level tool used to examine the broader external environment.
- **Porter's Five Forces framework**: is a micro tool for examining the industry in which an organization competes.
- **Priority**: Represents the organization's major areas of focus, through which key outputs are produced using capabilities.
- **Process Re-engineering**: Method of analysis & redesign of workflows within and between enterprises

to streamline work processes & achieve improvement in quality, time management, costs.

- **Program**: is a set of related projects managed in a coordinated way, which we qualified with to achieve benefits or synergy that cannot be achieved by managing them individually.
- **Project**: is a temporary endeavor undertaken to deliver a unique product, service, or result. A project has a definite scope, specific start and completion dates, and a distinct cost.
- **Rolling Forecast**: budget method that allows an organization to continually adjust to changing conditions by revisiting targets, generally on a quarterly basis, as opposed to a yearly cycle.
- **Scorecards**: A collection of key performance indicators (KPIs) and objectives, possibly arranged hierarchically. Scorecards are used to measure multiple facets of organization performance.
- **Sector**: A wide ranging area of interest, in which government aspires to achieve specific goals and outcomes for the community.
- **Six Sigma**: Systematic, data-driven methodology using tools, training, measurements to enable product/ process design that meets customer expectations and can be produced at Six Sigma levels quality levels; emphasis on reduction of process variation.
- **Stakeholder**: A person, group or organization to which an entity is accountable, or a person, group or organization affected by the actions of an Entity.
- **Strategic Area:** A major strategic thrust for the organization, such as maximizing shareholder value or improving the efficiency of operations.
- **Strategic initiative**: is an integrated set of programs and/or projects managed in a coordinated way and aimed at building core or differentiating business capability.

- **Strategic Outcome**: Are outcomes pitched at a high level, long term, focused and aligned with goal and can be linked to specific outputs. Strategic outcomes may have external comparative measures and some measures will be determined by internationally accepted procedures.
- **Strategic Planning Framework**: A policy structure that facilitates high level long term planning.
- **Strategy Map**: Provides a visual representation to illustrate the cause and effect relationship between strategic goals and the processes that organization use to achieve them.
- **Strategy:** Statements of major approach or method (the means) for attaining broad goals and resolving specific issues. It is an integrated set of choices that position a firm, in an industry, to earn superior returns over the long run.
- **Sub-Sector**: A further breakdown of a sector into its composite areas and for which subordinate goals and outcomes can be set.
- **SWOT analysis**: is mostly used by organizations to know their Strengths, Weaknesses, Opportunities, and Threats.
- **Target:** An expected level of performance or improvement required in the future. The current estimate of future result to be achieved by a given date. There may be multiple targets over time for the same measure.
- **Textual Analysis**: Analysis of the frequency, semantic relationships, and relative importance of particular terms, phrases and documents in online texts.
- **The Value Chain**: sequence and configuration of business activities that deliver value to customers.
- **Total Quality Management:** Management strategy aimed at embedding quality awareness in all

organizational processes to create continual increase in customer satisfaction at continually lower real costs.

- **Value Based Management**: addresses the value of a company which is determined by its discounted future cash flows. It focuses on how a company uses value to make both major strategic and everyday operating decisions.
- **Vision**: An overall statement of how the organization wants to be perceived over the long-term. It represents the overarching purpose that guides the long term decision-making processes. It is both aspirational and inspirational in nature.
- **Yield Analysis**: Employing basic statistics to understand yield volume, quality and to compare one batch of items with another. Often displayed visually.

FOR FURTHER READING

❖ ❖ ❖

VI. FOR FURTHER READING

- Ackroyd, S., & Hughes, J., 1983. Data collection in context. Harlow: Longman. pp. 66
- Alan Carpenter MLA, Better Planning Better Future - A Framework for Strategic Management for Western Australia, 9/1/2006, Premier Office, pp.4-12
- Allam Schofield, What Can Performance Measurement and Key Performance Indicators Do For Higher Education Institutions - a UK Perspective, Leadership Foundation for Higher Education
- Andrew J. Pateman,, Five easy steps for developing your BSC measures, 4/1/2004, Balanced Scorecard Report, pp.15-17
- Ann Nevius, How Healthcare Organizations can use the BSC to Succeed, 6/1/2001, Balanced Scorecard Collaborative
- Anne Field, Toward a More Perfect Union: How OSMs Supported Integration at Sprint Nextel, 10/1/2008, Balanced Scorecard Report, pp.10-12
- Antosh Nirmul, Strategy Focused Business Planning, 9/1/2004, Balanced Scorecard Collaborative
- Armstrong, J.S & Overton, T.S. 1977, `estimating non-response bias in mail surveys', Journal of Marketing Research, vol. 14, pp. 396-402.
- Arthur M. Schneiderman, How to Build a BSC - The Strategic Planning Process, pp.2-24
- Arthur Schneiderman, Why BSC Fail, 1/1/1999, Journal of Strategic Performance Measurement, pp.6-10
- Audit Commission, Delivering Improvement Together, 11/1/2001, Audit Commission, pp.3-68
- Auditor General Office, Auditor General Report - Fourth - Public Sector Performance Report 2007, 9/1/2007, Auditor General for Western Australia

- Australian Government, Transport Outputs and Programmes - Annual Report 2006, 12/1/2006, Department of Transport and Regional Services
- Balanced Scorecard Collaborative, QPR ScoreCard, 1/1/2004, QPR Software Plc
- Balancing Measures - Best Practices in Performance Management, 8/1/1999, The National Partnership for Reinventing Government (NPR), pp.5-57
- Barbara Minto, The Pyramid Principle, by Financial Times, 2002
- Basingstoke and Deane, Policy And Performance Management Framework, 12/7/2008, , pp.3-8
- Bernard Marr and Andy Neely, Automating the balanced scorecard – selection criteria to identify appropriate software applications, VOL. 7 2003, Measuring Business Excellence , pp.29-36
- Berwyne Jones, Strategic Planning in Government - The Key to Reinventing Ourselves, 2/1/1996, PM, pp.12-15
- Beyond Budgeting - SAP, 1/1/2001, SAP Software
- Bill Ravensberg, From Golf to Balanced Scorecards, pp.1-9
- Bisher Jardaneh, Using BSC to Drive Break throught Performance - Arabtech Jordan, 3/1/2008, Arabtech Jordan
- Board Committee on System Strategic Planning, Planning Framework Developed by the Strategic Planning Work Group, 10/18/2002, Oregon State Board of Higher Education, pp.4-26
- Bob Paladino, Integrating Balanced Scorecards with Human Capital Compensation - Rewards and Recognition Programs to Drive Value, , Balanced Scorecard Collaborative, pp.1-7
- Brenda Moncla and Marianne Arents-Gregory, Corporate Performance Management - Turning Strategy Into Action, , DM Review, pp.1-5

- Brett Knowles, Five Distinct Views of Scorecards and Their Implications, , Performance Measurement Solutions, pp.2-4
- Brett Knowles, The 5 Simple Steps to Building an Award-Winning Balanced Scorecard, , Balanced Scorecard Collaborative, pp.1-6
- Brian Baker, Mobil NAMR, , Balanced Scorecard Collaborative, pp.3-17
- British Quality Foundation (BQF)., The European framework – the EFQM Excellence Model, 1/1/1999, Department of Trade and Industry – UK, pp.1-3
- Bruce C Hartnett, Secretaries Performance Reviews, 8/1/2007, State Services Authority
- Bryman, A., 1989. Research methods and organization studies. London: Routledge
- Bulmer, M., 1986. The role of theory on applied social science. In C. Weiss (Ed.), Social science and social policy. London: George Allen and Unwin
- Burns, R. B., 2000. Introduction to research methods. London: Sage Publications Ltd
- Business Management Solution, Strategy Management - Business Management Solution, 1/1/2004, Solution Portals, pp.3-9
- Business Objects, Business Objects: Raising the Bar on Itself with Analytic Applications, 1/1/2002, Aberdeen Group
- Buytendijk, Frank and Rayner, Nigel. "A Starter's Guide to CPM Methodologies." Gartner, May 2002.
- Cassandra Frangos, Aligning Human Capital to Organization Strategy, 1/1/2005, Balanced Scorecard Collaborative
- Cassandra Frangos, Motivate - Align Personal Objectives, 4/1/2003, Balanced Scorecard Collaborative
- CFO Research Services and Comshare, Incorporated, What CFOs Want from Performance Management, March 2003, pp.6

- Char LaBounty, Service Level Management - An Overview, , LaBounty & Associates, Inc, pp.1-4
- Chris Bragg, Successfully Implementing Strategic Activity - Project Portfolio Management - The missing link, 3/8/2008, 2GC Active Management
- Christiane Arndt and Charles Oman, Uses and Abuses of Governance Indicators, 1/1/2006, Development Centre Studies
- Christopher D. Ittner, David F. Larcker, and Marshall W. Meyer, Performance, Compensation and The BSC - phd, 11/1/1997, The Wharton School - The University of Pennsylvania
- CIO Insight/Balanced Scorecard Collaborative (BSCol), Society for Human Resource Management (SHRM)/BSCol study, 2002
- Cook, T. D., Campbell, D. T., & Peracchio, L., 1990. Quasi experimentation. In M. Hough (Ed.), Handbook of Industrial and Organizational Psychology Palo Alto, CA: Consulting Psychologists Press, Inc., Vol. 1, pp. 491-576
- Cristian Mitreanu, Strategy Redefined, 1/1/2004, RedefiningStrategy.com
- D. P. Norton and J. R. Weiser, "The Strategy Review Process," BSR November–December 2006
- Dana Goldblatt, Use Strategic Communications to Execute Strategy - Why Strategic Communications Is So Critical, , Balanced Scorecard Collaborative
- Daniel Kaufmann and Aart Kraay, On Measuring Governance - Issues for Debate, 1/1/2007, The World Bank
- Daniel Meade, The Art and Science of Measurement: The Nature of Indicators on the Balanced Scorecard, , Tec de Monterrey, pp.2-8
- Davenport, T and Harris, J.., Competing on analytics: The New Science of Winning, Harvard Business School Press, 2007

- David Norton, Creating The New Office Of Strategy Management - BSC 2008 Form, 3/1/2008, Palladium
- David P. Norton and Randall H. Russell,, Motivate to Make Strategy Everyone's Job, 12/1/2004, Balanced Scorecard Report, pp.2-5
- David P. Norton and Randall H. Russell,, Assessment to make strategy execution a core competency, 10/1/2005, Balanced Scorecard Report, pp.2-5
- David P. Norton and Randall H. Russell,, Govern to Make Strategy a continual process, 2/1/2006, Balanced Scorecard Report, pp.2-5
- David P. Norton and Randall H. Russell,, Translate the Strategy into Operational Terms, 6/1/2006, Balanced Scorecard Report, pp.2-6
- David P. Norton, Linking Strategy and Planning to budgets - Part 1, Vol 8 # 3 2006, Balanced Scorecard Report, pp.1-6
- David P. Norton, Philip W. Peck,, Linking Operations to Strategy and Budgeting, 10/1/2008, Balanced Scorecard Report, pp.1-6
- David P. Norton,, Linking Strategy and Planning to Budgets, 6/1/2006, Balanced Scorecard Report, pp.2-6
- Denise Lindsey Wells, Strategic Management for Senior Leaders - A Handbook for Implementation, 3/1/1996, Department of the Navy Total Quality Leadership Office, pp.3-94
- Dennis Campbell,, Choose the right measures and drive the right strategy, 6/1/2006, Balanced Scorecard Report, pp.14-16
- Dennis Koci, Defining and Executing Strategy - The Balance Scorecard - Hilton, 3/3/2008, Hilton Hotel Corp.
- Denzin, N. K., 1989. The research act: A theoretical introduction to sociological methods (3rd ed.). Englewood Cliffs, NJ: Prentice Hall.

- Department of Administrative Services, Performance Measure Guidelines For Oregon State Agencies, 9/1/2007, Oregon State , pp.C1-27
- Department of Infrastructure, Best Practice Guidelines - Local Government Entity - Audit Committees & Internal Audit, 6/1/2000, Australian Accounting Research Foundation
- Department of Premier and Cabinet, Certification of Performance Indicator - Annual Report 2005-2006, 6/1/2006, Australian Government
- Department of the Attorney General, Department of the Attorney General - Annual Report 2005-2006, 12/1/2006, Government of Western Australia
- Department of the Premier and Cabinet, Business Performance Management, 1/6/2006, The State of Queensland - Queensland Government
- Department of Transport and Regional Services, Department of Transport and Regional Services - Annual Report 2005-2006, 1/1/2006, Commonwealth of Australia 2006
- Department of Treasury and Finance , Outcome Based Management, 11/1/2004, Government of Western Australia, pp.8-23
- Dept of Trade and Industry, Performance Measurement,, UK Government, pp.1-7
- Dept. of Finance, Strategic Planning Guidelines - California State, 3/1/1998, California State Government, pp.6-44
- Dept. of Treasury and Finance, -Treasury and Finance - Quarterly financial statement - Mar 2007, 3/1/2007, Western Australia Government
- Derar Almanaseer, Introducing a New Way of Thinking - Case Study, 3/4/2008, Ministry of Public Works and Housing
- Diane Johnson , PeopleSoft EDW and EPM Solution Overview, 4/1/1999, Data Warehouse Service Line

- Diaz Nesamoney, SaaS - Finally a BI Model for the Masses, 3/1/2007, DM Review, pp.2-9
- Downward, P., Finch, J. H., & Ramsay, J., 2002. Critical realism, empirical methods and inference: A critical discussion. Cambridge Journal of Economics, 26, pp. 481- 500.
- Dr Okan Geray , Dubai eGovernement - Strategy Map and BSC, 3/5/2008, Dubai eGovernement
- Dr. David Norton, Beware - The Unbalanced Scorecard, 4/1/2002, Balanced Scorecard Form, pp.27-30
- Dr. David Norton, The Corporate Scorecard - Making the whole more than the sum of its parts, 2/1/2000, Balanced Scorecard Form, pp.21-26
- Dr. David Norton, Use Strategy Maps to Communicate Strategy, 12/1/1999, Balanced Scorecard Form, pp.3-8
- Dr. David Norton, When a Scorecard is not a Scorecard, 2/1/2000, Balanced Scorecard Form, pp.17-20
- Dr. David Norton, BSC Basics - Getting it Right, 4/1/2000, Balanced Scorecard Form, pp.1-2
- Dr. David Norton, Describing and Measuring Organizational Capital, 7/1/2004, Balanced Scorecard Collaborative
- Dr. David Norton, Linking Strategy to Operation - The New Management System, 3/1/2008, Balanced Scorecard Form
- Dr. David Norton, Organization Alignment - A Prerequisite for Executing Strategy, 2/1/2006, NetConference
- Dr. Robert Kaplan & David Norton, Having Trouble With Your Strategy Then Map It, 10/1/2000, Harvard Business Review, pp. 7-13
- Dr. Robert Kaplan & David Norton, Integrated Strategy Planning and Operational Execution A Six-Stage System, 6/1/2008, Balanced Scorecard Report, pp.2-6

- Dr. Robert Kaplan & David Norton, Mastering the Management System, 1/1/2008, Harvard Business Review, pp.3-17
- Dr. Robert Kaplan & David Norton, Strategic Management - An Emerging Profession, 1/25/2004, Balanced Scorecard Collaborative, pp.1-4
- Dr. Robert Kaplan & David Norton, Approaches for Implementation - BSC 2008 Form, 3/1/2008, Palladium
- Dr. Robert Kaplan & David Norton, Having Trouble With Your Strategy Then Map It, 10/1/2000, Harvard Business Review, pp.7-13
- Dr. Robert Kaplan & David Norton, Integrated Strategy Planning and Operational Execution A Six-Stage System, 6/1/2008, Balanced Scorecard Report, pp.2-6
- Dr. Robert Kaplan & David Norton, Linking Strategy to Planning and Budgeting, 1/1/2000, Harvard Business School, pp.3-5
- Dr. Robert Kaplan & David Norton, Mastering the Management System, 1/1/2008, Harvard Business Review, pp.3-17
- Dr. Robert Kaplan & David Norton, Strategic Job Families, 12/1/2003, Harvard Business School, pp.2-15
- Dr. Robert Kaplan & David Norton, Strategic Management - An Emerging Profession, 1/25/2004, Balanced Scorecard Collaborative,, pp.1-4
- Dr. Robert Kaplan & Marvin Bower, Overcoming the Barriers to BSC use in the Public Sector, , Harvard Business Review, pp.10-11
- Dr. Robert Kaplan & Marvin Bower, The Balanced Scorecard - Measures That Drive Performance, 2/2/1992, Harvard Business Review, pp.72-79
- Dr. Robert Kaplan & Marvin Bower, The Balanced Scorecard for Public-Sector Organizations, , In Context, pp.10-12

- Dr. Robert Kaplan & Marvin Bower, Using The BSC As a Strategic Management System, 2/1/1996, Harvard Business Review, pp.75-85
- Dr. Robert Kaplan, Can Bad Things Happen to BSC, 10/1/1999, Balanced Scorecard Form, pp.9-12
- Dr. Robert Kaplan, Can Bad Things Happen to good BSC - Part II of Implementation Pitfalls, 10/1/1999, Balanced Scorecard Form, pp.13-16
- Dr. Robert Kaplan, City of Charlotte, 2005, Harvard Business School Publishing, pp.1-13
- Dr. Robert Kaplan, Nova Scotia Power, 2005, Balanced Scorecard Collaborative, pp.3-13
- Dr. Robert Kaplan, Royal Canadian Mounted police, 2005, Harvard Business School Publishing, pp.1-15
- Dr. Robert Kaplan, Tennessee Valley Authority, 2005, Harvard Business School Publishing, pp.1-18
- Dr. Robert Kaplan, Using Strategic Themes to Achieve Organizational Alignment, 11/1/2001, Harvard Business School, pp.3-7
- Dr. Robert Kaplan, BSC Form – Dubai, Middle East 2008
- Dylan Miyake, Implementing Strategy with the Balanced Scorecard: An Introduction to the Strategy-Focused Organization, , DM Review, pp.1-4
- Easterby-Smith, M., Thorpe, R. & Lowe, A. 1991, Management Research: an Introduction, Sage, London pp. 31
- Easterby-Smith, M., Thorpe, R., & Lowe, A., 2002. Management research: An introduction (2nd ed.). London: Sage Publications Ltd
- Economic And Social Commission For Asia And The Pacific, Guidelines on Strategic Planning and Management of the Energy Sector, 1/1/2002, United Nations - New York, pp.1-73
- Economic Policy Division, Labour Force Statistics - Key Results – Western Australia, 5/1/2007, Australian Government

- Elaine Brennan, Aligning the Culture of a BSC company, 2/1/2002, Balanced Scorecard Collaborative
- Elizabeth Kohlenberg, Washington State Health BSC - Accountability ScoreCard, 7/1/2003, Washington State Health Dept.
- Enterprise Planning: Linking Strategies, Plans And Resources For Competitive Advantage, 6/27/1905, Hyperion
- Eric Beinhocker & Sarah Kaplan, Tired of Strategic Planning, 2002 Number 2, The McKinsey Quarterly, pp.1-7
- Eric Beinhocker & Sarah Kaplan, Tired of Strategic Planning, 2002 Number 2, The McKinsey Quarterly, pp.1-7
- Erik Öhman, Performance Management in Nordea, , Nordea
- Eshaq Jaberi, Exploring Almajdouie Group's Journey in implementing BSC in a diversified organization, 3/6/2008, Almajdouie Group
- Exerpted from BSC Hall of Fame Report, Economic Development Administration (US), 2005, Harvard Business School Publishing, pp.1-2
- Fey, C. F., & Denison, D. R., 2003. Organizational culture and effectiveness: Can American theory be applied in Russia? Organization Science, 14(6), pp. 686-706.
- Fey, C. F., & Denison, D. R., 2003. Organizational culture and effectiveness: Can American theory be applied in Russia? Organization Science, pp.686-706
- Fielding, N. G., & Fielding, J. L., 1986. Linking data. Beverley Hills: Sage Publications Ltd
- Finn, M., Elliot-White, M., & Walton, M., 2000. Tourism and Leisure Research
- Fischer, F., 1998. Beyond empiricism: Policy inquiry in postpositivist perspective. Policy Studies Journal, 26(1), pp. 129-146.

- Francesco Zingales & Kai Hockerts, BSC & Sustainability - Examples from literature and practice, 1/3/2003, Centre for the Management of Environmental Resources, pp.1-11
- Frank Martinelli, Strategic Planning in Nonprofit and Public Sector Organizations, 1/1/1999, The Center for Public Skills Training, pp.28-35
- G. Lawrie, D. Kalff, & H. Andersen, Integrating Risk Management with existing methods of strategic control - Avoiding Duplication within the Corporate Governance agenda, 8/1/2003, 2GC Active Management, pp.8-16
- Gable, G.G. 1994, `Integrating case study and survey research methods: an example in information systems', European Journal of Information Systems, vol. 3, no. 2, pp. 112-126.
- Gary Hamel and C.K. Prahalad, Competing for the Future, Harvard Business School Press, 1994, pp. 120-121
- Gavin Lawrie, Integrating Risk and Performance Management, 6/1/2004, 2GC Active Management
- Georgia M. Harrigan and Ruth E. Miller, Managing Change Through an Aligned and Cascading Balanced Scorecard- A Case Study, , Naval Undersea Warfare Center Division
- Glenberg, A., & Langston, W., 1992. Comprehension of illustrated text: Pictures help to build mental models. Journal of Memory & Language, 31, pp.129-151
- Glenn, Senator John, excerpt from opening statements – United States Senate Committee on Governmental Affairs "Improving Government Performance and Organization, 1993, as cited in An Overview of Performance Measurement, ICMA/Richard Fisher, ICMA website, USA, 2001

- Gomez-Mejia, L. R., 1994. Executive compensation: A reassessment and a future research agenda. Personnel and Human Resources Management, pp.161-222
- Graeme Doyle, Department of Corrective Services - Annual Report 2006, 9/1/2006, Department of Corrective Services
- Grant Hehir, Department Of Treasury And Finance - Annual Report 2005-2006 b, 12/1/2006, Dept. of Treasury and Finance
- Guidelines for Implementing Balanced Scorecard, 1/1/2001, QPR Software, pp.4-9
- Guy Weismantel, An Enterprise Approach to Performance Management, 6/26/2005, Business Objects,
- Hassard, J. 1990, `Multiple paradigms and organizational analysis: a case study', Organizational Studies, vol. 12, issue 2, pp. 275-299
- Henrik Andersen, Gavin Lawrie, and Michael Shulver, The Balanced Scorecard vs. The EFQM Business Excellence Model, 6/1/2000, 2GC Active Management, pp.2-14
- Henry Mintzberg, The Pitfalls Of Strategic Planning, Fall, 1993, California Management Review,, pp.1-12
- Henry Mintzberg, Bruce Ahlstrand and Joseph Lampel. Strategy Safari: A guided tour through the wilds of strategic management, 1998, Free Press, New York
- Henry Morris, Policy Hubs - Linking analytic and operational applications, 6/30/2008, InContext
- Hinton, P. R., 1995. Statistics explained. A guide for social science students. London: Routledge
- Holland, P. W., 1986. Statistics and causal inference. Journal of the American Statistical Association, pp.945-960.
- Howard Rohm, A Balancing Act, Vol 2 Issue 2, Reform Magazine, pp.1-8

- Hsiao, C., 2003. Analysis of panel data (2nd ed.). Cambridge: Cambridge University Press
- Hussey, J., & Hussey, R., 1997. Business research: A practical guide for undergraduate and postgraduate students. London: McMillan Press Ltd.
- Ian Cobbold & Gavin Lawrie, Classification of Balanced Scorecards based on their intended use, 5/1/2002, PMA Conference - Boston, pp.1-8
- Ian Cobbold & Gavin Lawrie, The Development of the Balanced Scorecard as a strategic management tool, 5/1/2002, PMA Conference - Boston, pp.1-9
- Ian Macdonald, Balance Scorecard - The Gateway to Business Performance Management - Microsoft, 3/7/2008, Microsoft Corporation
- Imagine Calagary Group, Imagine Calagary Plan for Long Range Urban Sustainability, 9/1/2007, The City of Calgary, pp.1-10
- Independent Pricing and Regulatory Tribunal (IPART), Benchmarking Local Government Performance in New South Wales – An Issues Paper, NSW Government, Australia, 1997
- Jacqueline Coolidge and Marc-A. Meunier, Making Enterprise Dashboards and Scorecards a Success, 2/1/2005, AMR Research, pp.1-12
- James Coffey, Three Steps to Successful Measures, 6/1/2005, Balanced Scorecard Report, pp.14-15
- Jan Rivkin, "Where do great strategies come from?" Harvard Business School Faculty Seminar Series Lecture
- Jane Brockington, Growing Victoria Together: The Victorian Whole of Government Strategic Framework , 8/1/2007, Department of Premier and Cabinet - Victoria
- Jane Mills, Building and Developing The Finance BSC - Diageo, 1/1/2000, Business Intelligence, pp.24-35
- Janice Koch, The challenge of target setting, 8/1/2007, Balanced Scorecard Report, pp.14-16

- Janice Koch, Alterra Health Cares Fast Track to Results, '2001, Balanced Scorecard Report, pp.23-24
- Jason Kuo, Management Dashboards Enabling Performance Management across the Enterprise, 10/1/2002, Business Objects
- Jeff Clements & Arun Dhingra, How to Launch your BSC program - Making the case at the executive level, 2/1/2004, Balanced Scorecard Collaborative
- Jeremy Hope and Robin Fraser, Beyond Budgeting - Q & A, 10/1/2001, Beyond Budgeting Round Table, pp.3-28
- Jick, T. D., 1979. Mixing qualitative and quantitative methods: Triangulation in action. Administrative Science Quarterly, pp. 24, 602-611.
- John H. Lingle, From BSC to IS Measurement, 1/1/2007, Wm. Schiemann & Associates Inc, pp.1-6
- John Hagerty, William McNeill, Business Objects XI Release 2 - A New Riff on Ease of Use, 10/1/2005, AMR Research
- John Wilkes, Corporate Governance and Measuring Performance, , SAS UK, pp.1-3
- John Wilkes, Performance Management, 1/1/2004, Capgemini
- Jon Meliones, Make Strategy Everyone's Job, 1/1/2001, Balanced Scorecard Collaborative
- Julián Maganto, Increasing the competitiveness of the Spanish Port System through the Balanced Scorecard, 6/1/2005, Puerto del Estado
- Justin Pettit, EVA and Strategy, 4/1/2000, Stern Stewart Europe Limited, pp.2-19
- Justin Pettit, EVA Client Comments, 4/1/2000, Stern Stewart Europe Limited, pp.2-4
- Katherine Kane, City of Brisbane - Corporate Strategy Map, 2004, Harvard Business School Publishing, pp.1-3
- Katherine Kane, City of Brisbane, 2004, Harvard Business School Publishing, pp.7-9

- Keith Gile, The Forrester Wave - BI Reporting And Analysis Platforms, 2/1/2006, Forrester
- Keith Hammonds, You've got to make time for strategy, 3/1/2001, Illustrations, pp.1-6
- Keith Katz, Travis Manzione, Maximize Your "Return on Initiatives" with the initiative portfolio review process, 6/1/2008, Balanced Scorecard Report, pp.2-16
- Kevin McCarthy, Achieving Balanced Regional Development - IDA Ireland, 8/1/2007, IDA Ireland
- Larry B. Weinstein and Joseph F. Castellano, Scorecard Support, pp.1-5
- László Pintér, Peter Hardi And Peter Bartelmus, Sustainable Development Indicators - UN, 12/1/2005, United Nations Division for Sustainable Development, pp.5-25
- Lauren Keller Johnson, KeyCorp: Executing a Customer Intimacy Strategy with the BSC, 10/1/2008, Balanced Scorecard Report, pp.7-9
- Lauren Keller Johnson,, Linking Strategic Planning and the Rolling Financial Forecast at Millipore, 6/1/2007, Balanced Scorecard Report, pp.11-13
- Laurie Burney McWhorter, Does the Balanced Scorecard Reduce Information Overload, Summer 2003 Vol 4 No 4, Management Accounting Quarterly, pp.23-27
- Lawrence G. Hrebiniak, Organizational Dynamics, "Obstacles to Effective Strategy Implementation" vol. 35, No. 1, 2006
- Lawrence P. Grayson, An Example - A Management Strategy for a Private School, 1/1/2004, Balanced Scorecard Institute, pp.1-8
- Lewis-Beck, M. S., 1993. Regression analysis (Vol. 2). London: Sage Publication Ltd.
- Luc Bossyns , Setting up a result-oriented organization, Aquafin

- M C Wauchope, Department of the Premier and Cabinet - Annual Report 2005-2006, 9/1/2006, Department of the Premier and Cabinet
- Malcolm Spiers, Keeping your BSC current - Zamil Group, 3/7/2008, Zamil Group
- Marilyn Michaels , Executing your strategy by ensuring company wide, bottom up, employee involvement in strategy formulation, 3/7/2008, Ricoh Corporation
- Marita Vos PhD, Communication quality measurement of Councils, Research Group Governmental Communication
- Mark Cashion, Balanced Scorecard Basics, 1/1/2008, Balanced Scorecard Collaborative
- Mark Cashion, BSCol Best-of-the-Best Public and Private Sector - Examples Strategy Maps, 3/1/2008, Balanced Scorecard Collaborative
- Mark Cashion, Concept paper on PMF Models for Government, 2/1/2008, Palladium
- Mark Cashion, Driving Alignment to Executing and implementing Qatar's long term vision - A Strategic Management Framework , 1/1/2008, Balanced Scorecard Collaborative
- Mark Shinder & David McDowell, ABC, The Balanced Scorecard and EVA - Distinguishing the Means from the End, 4/1/1999, Stern Stewart Europe Limited, pp.2-7
- Marlyse Lipe and Steven Salterio, "A Note On The Judgemental Effects Of The Balanced Scorecard S Information Organization," Accounting, Organizations and Society, 2002, pp. 531-540
- Matt H. Evans,, Course 11: The Balanced Scorecard, 2/1/2002, Excellence in Financial Management, pp.2-38
- McNeill, P., 1990. Research methods (2nd ed.). London: Routledge.

- Members of Quality Scotland, The EFQM Excellence Model & Balanced Scorecard, 2/1/2007, Quality Scotland, pp.1-4
- Methods: Data collection, analysis and interpretation. London: Longman
- Michael Nagel & Chris Rigatuso, Improving Corporate Governance: A Balanced Scorecard Approach, 1/1/2003, Balanced Scorecard Collaborative, pp.4-11
- MicroStrategy Incorporated, Bi Market Consolidation: Re-Igniting The Debate Of Open Systems Vs. Closed Systems, 1/1/2007, MicroStrategy Incorporated, pp.2-8
- Mike Wisniewski, The Measures of Success - Developing a BSC to measure performance, 6/1/1998, Accounts Commission for Scotland, pp.5-7
- Miyake, Dylan. "Implementing Strategy with the Balanced Scorecard: An Introduction to the Strategy-Focused Organization." DM Review, October 2002
- National Institute of Standards and Technology, who administer the Baldridge award
- Neil McDougall & André Ribeiro Coutinho, Promoting Economic Development: Strategic Agendas in Action, 12/1/2007, BSC Report, pp.14-16
- Neil McDougall and André Ribeiro Coutinho, Promoting Economic Development: Strategic Agendas in Action, , Balanced Scorecard Report, pp.14-16
- Nigel Rayner, Magic Quadrant for CPM Suites 2007, 12/1/2007, Gartner, pp.2-11
- Office of the Auditor General for Western Australia, Audit Practice Statement - Australia, 12/1/2007, Auditor General for Western Australia
- Office of the Auditor General for Western Australia, Public Sector Performance Indicators 1993-1994, 12/1/1994, Western Australia Government
- Osborne, D. & Gaebler, R., Reinventing Government, 1992

- Ostle, B., & Malone, L. C., 1988. Statistics in research: Basic concepts and techniques for research workers (4th ed.). Iowa, IO: Iowa State University Press
- Palladium BSC Master Class Handbook 2008
- Palladium Group Report, 2007
- Pam Syfert, City of Charlotte, Balanced Scorecard Collaborative, pp.3-14
- Parkhe, A. 1993, `"Messy" research, methodological predispositions, and theory development in international joint ventures', Academy of Management Review, vol. 18, no. 2, pp. 227-268.
- Pat Dinan, Balanced Scorecard as a post – merger integration tool, , Conoco Phillips North Sea
- Patricia Bush and Diane Koziel, How and why to build an internal marketing campaign, 1/1/2007, Balanced Scorecard Collaborative, pp.7-9
- Paul D. Hamerman, Business Objects Assembles A Leading Product Set In Business Performance Solutions, 10/1/2007, Forrester
- Paul D. Hamerman, Business Objects Assembles A Leading Product Set In Business Performance Solutions, 10/1/2007, Forrester
- Paul R. Niven, Balanced Scorecard Step by Step - Maximizing Performance and Maintaining Results
- Paul R. Niven, Cascading the BSC - a case study on Nova Scotia power
- Paul R. Niven, Primerus Consulting, Adapting The Balanced Scorecard To Fit The Public And Nonprofit Sectors, 4/22/2003, QPR, pp.2-5
- Pavlik, E. L., Scott, T. W., & Tiessen, P., 1993. Executive's compensation: Issues and research. Journal of Accounting Literature pp.131-189
- Penny Armytage, Department of Justice - Annual Report 2005-2006, 12/1/2006, Victoria - Australia
- Performance Management, Strategy Management and the Balanced Scorecard, 4/1/2007, GEAC

- Perry, C. & Coote, L. 1994, `Processes of a cases study research methodology: tool for management development?', Australia and New Zealand Association for Management Annual Conference, Victoria University of Wellington, New Zealand
- Peter Bunce & Robin Fraser, Beyond Budgeting, 6/1/2002, Beyond Budgeting Round Table, pp.5-16
- Peter LaCasse, Initiative Management - Putting Strategy into Action, 12/1/2007, Performance Management, pp.7-13
- Phil Aisthorpe, Linking the Balanced Scorecard to Corporate Strategy, 9/1/1997, Halifax plc.
- Philip Howard, BusinessObjects Data Integrator XI - Release 2, 1/1/2006, Bloor Research
- Philip Kirby & Sumner J. Schmiesing, Balanced Scorecards as Strategic Navigational Charts - How to Implement Rapid Sustainable Change, 4/1/2003, Organization Thoughtware International & Visum Solutions, Inc., 1-11"
- Philip Kirby & Sumner J. Schmiesing, Balanced Scorecards as Strategic Navigational Charts - How to Implement Rapid Sustainable Change, 4/1/2003, Organization Thoughtware International & Visum Solutions, Inc., pp.1-11
- Philip Peck,, Leveraging Planning Processes to Bridge Strategy and Execution, 1/1/2007, Palladium Strategy Execution, pp.1-12
- Primal Leadership - The Hidden Driver of Great Performance, CMA Canada
- Public Affairs Manager – Federal Magistrates Court of Australia, Federal Magistrates Court Of Australia - Annual Report 2006-2007, 12/1/2007, Australian Government
- R Atkinson,, Performance Management Strategy 2007, 1/1/2007, Eden District Council, pp.3-14

- R. S. Kaplan and R. Cooper; Cost & Effect; Harvard Business School Press, Boston Massachusetts 1998. pp.197
- R. S. Kaplan, "The Demise of Cost and Profit Centers," BSR January–February 2007
- Randall Russell, Luxfur Gas Cylinders - Mastering the Strategy - Operations Linkage, 6/1/2008, Balanced Scorecard Report, pp.7-13
- Rayner, Nigel. "CPM: A Strategic Deployment of BI Applications." Gartner, May 2002
- Remenyi, D., Williams, B., Money, A., & Swartz, E., 1998. Doing research in business and management: An introduction to process and method. London: Sage Publications Ltd.
- Richard D. Young, Perspectives on Strategic Planning in the Public Sector, 1/1/2003, Governmental Research with the Institute for Public Service and Policy Research, pp.1-28
- Robert Kaplan , Strategy Execution - BSC 2008 Form, 3/1/2008, Palladium
- Robert Gold, Using the Balanced Scorecard to Enable the Strategy-Focused IT Organization, 5/1/2001, Balanced Scorecard Collaborative
- Robert L. Howie, and Randall H. Russell, Best Practices of Hall of Fame Organizations, 4/1/2004, Balanced Scorecard Collaborative
- Robert Mellor, Performance Measurement & Management In Asian-Pacific Local Government, 9/1/2003, The Network of Local Government Training and Research, pp.2-69
- Robert S. Kaplan and Anthony A. Atkinson. Advanced Management Accounting, 3rd edition, Prentice Hall, Upper Saddle River, N.J., 1998.
- Robert S. Kaplan and David P. Norton, Organization Capital - Supporting the Change Agenda That Supports Strategy Execution, , Balanced Scorecard Collaborative

- Robert S. Kaplan and Michael E. Nagel, Improving Corporate Governance with the Balanced Scorecard, 3/1/2004, NACD – Directors Monthly, pp.16-20
- Robert S. Kaplan, Communication and Education to Make Strategy Everyone's Job, 6/22/2005, Harvard Business Review, pp.3-6
- Robert S. Kaplan, "Overcoming the Barriers to Balanced Scorecard Use in the Public Sector," Balanced Scorecard Report, Nov/Dec 2002
- Robert S. Kaplan, "The Balanced Scorecard and Nonprofit Organizations," Balanced Scorecard Report, November-December, 2002. pp. 1-4.
- Robert S. Kaplan, Target Setting, 6/1/2006, Balanced Scorecard Report, pp.10-13
- Robert S. Kaplan, Using Strategic Themes to Achieve Organizational Alignment, , Balanced Scorecard Collaborative
- Rod Glover, Setting the National Agenda - The National Reform Agenda, 8/1/2007, Department of Premier and Cabinet - Victoria
- Roland Baumann, Strategic Management -Turning Concept into Reality, 6/1/2005, Serono
- Russom, Philip. "Five Easy Pieces." Intelligent Enterprise, October 8, 2002. Copyright CMP Media LLC.
- Samson Samasoni, Effective Internal Communications - ADGSEC, 11/1/2007, Bell Pottinger Middle East
- Samson Samasoni, How Do I Know My Communications Plan Is Working? Measurement and Monitoring, 11/2/2007, Bell Pottinger Middle East
- Sayer, A., 1992. Method in social science: A realist approach. London: Routledge
- Simon Lewis, Maximizing the Performance Excellence of Your Human Capital throught the BSC, 3/7/2008, Emirates Group

- Smith, Mark. "Business Planning or Business Performance Management?" Intelligent Enterprise, September 24, 2002.
- Stefan Gössler, What is the Right Performance Management Approach for Your Organization, , SAS
- Stein Helgeby, The role of budget in performance management, 8/1/2007, Victorian Department of Treasury and Finance
- Stephen Gates, Aligning Strategic Performance Measures and Results, 11/1/2001, Balanced Scorecard Interest Group
- Stern Stewart, EVA Metric Wars, 10/1/1996, The Magazine for Senior Financial Executives, pp.1-7
- Steve Bracks, Growing Victoria Together Vision, 3/1/2001, Premier Office of Victoria
- Steve Bracks, Victoria Goals Summary, 3/2/2001, Premier Office of Victoria
- Steve Johnson, EFQM and Balanced Scorecard - for improving organizational performance, 4/1/2003, INLAND REVENUE, pp.8-30
- Stoffels, J. Strategic Issues Management: A Comprehensive Guide to Environmental Scanning, Pergamon, 1994, pp.1.
- Strategic HR Management Systems, How is your HR Scorcard, 2/1/2003, ASL Consulting,, pp.1-3
- Strategy Map Telefónica S.A.- Aligning and engaging a complex organization around Group Strategy, 6/1/2005, BSC European Summit
- Stroh, M., 2000. Qualitative interviewing. In D. Burton (Ed.), Research training for social scientists. London: Sage Publications Ltd. pp. 196-214
- Ted Friedman, Mark A. Beyer, Andreas Bitterer, Magic Quadrant for Data Integration Tool, 10/1/2007, Gartner RAS Core Research, pp.2-30

- Terry Brown, How to mobilize the Executive Team for Strategic change - The SFO Readiness Assessment, 1/1/2002, Balanced Scorecard Collaborative, pp.3-5
- Terry S. Brown and Matthew R. Gill,, Charting New Horizons with Initiative Management, 10/1/2008, Balanced Scorecard Report, pp.13-16
- The City of Charlotte strategy-focused organization, Strategic Planning Handbook - Charlotte's Model for Integrating Budget and Performance Management, 10/1/2002, The City of Charlotte, pp.2-14
- The Economist Intelligence Unit (EIU) / Business Objects, 2007
- The International Bank for Reconstruction and Development , A Decade of Measuring the Quality of Governance - Gov Indicators 1996-2006 - World Bank, 12/1/2006, The World Bank
- The International Bank for Reconstruction and Development , World Bank Development Indicators - UAE, , The World Bank
- Timo Elliott, Choosing a Business Intelligence Standard, 1/1/2004, Business Objects
- Timothy Koller, What is value-based management, Vol 3 1994, The Mckinsey Quaterly, pp.87-100
- Timothy Marney, Department Of Treasury And Finance - Annual Report 2005-2006, 12/1/2006, Department Of Treasury And Finance
- Tobias Waldeck, Driving value with the SFO assessement, 2/1/2005, Balanced Scorecard Collaborative
- Travis Manzione,, Driving the new management meeting with technology, 4/1/2006, Balanced Scorecard Report, pp.15-16
- UN, - United Arab Emirates-The Human Development Index - going beyond income, 1/2/2006, UN

- UN, Human Development Report 2006, 1/1/2007, United Nations Development Programme
- UN, Human Development Report 2007-2008, 1/1/2008, United Nations Development Programme
- UN, The State if the World Children 2008 - Statistics Table, 1/1/2008, United Nations Development Program
- UN, -UNDP UAE Metrics Statistics, 1/1/2006, UN
- Venkatesh Ramaswamy , Making the Journey to the BSC - National Bank of Kuwait, 3/7/2008, National Bank of Kuwait
- Victoria Strategy & Indicator Progress - Yearly Report 2007-08, 1/1/2008, Victoria - Australia
- Web Conference, 3rd Generation BSC - Practical Improvements to Facilitate Implementation and Maximize success, 1/1/2004, 2GC Ltd.
- William Casey, Successful Strategy Implementation, pp.2-5
- William Fonvielle and Lawrence P. Carr, Gaining Alignment - Making Scorecards Work, 1/3/1999, Management Accounting, pp.1-12
- William Schiemann & John Lingle, Seven Greatest Myths Of Measurement, Metrus Group, pp.2-4
- Yin, R.K. 1989, Case Study Research Design and Methods, Sage, London, pp. 41

8374442R0

Made in the USA
Charleston, SC
03 June 2011